Beginning AWS Security

Build Secure, Effective, and Efficient AWS Architecture

Tasha Penwell

Apress®

Beginning AWS Security: Build Secure, Effective, and Efficient AWS Architecture

Tasha Penwell
Vinton, VA, USA

ISBN-13 (pbk): 978-1-4842-9680-6   ISBN-13 (electronic): 978-1-4842-9681-3
https://doi.org/10.1007/978-1-4842-9681-3

Managing Director, Apress Media LLC: Welmoed Spahr
Acquisitions Editor: Celestin Suresh John
Development Editor: James Markham
Coordinating Editor: Mark Powers

Cover designed by eStudioCalamar

Cover image by Kayeon Pixabay (www.pixabay.com)

Distributed to the book trade worldwide by Apress Media, LLC, 1 New York Plaza, New York, NY 10004, U.S.A. Phone 1-800-SPRINGER, fax (201) 348-4505, e-mail orders-ny@springer-sbm.com, or visit www.springeronline.com. Apress Media, LLC is a California LLC and the sole member (owner) is Springer Science + Business Media Finance Inc (SSBM Finance Inc). SSBM Finance Inc is a **Delaware** corporation.

For information on translations, please e-mail booktranslations@springernature.com; for reprint, paperback, or audio rights, please e-mail bookpermissions@springernature.com.

Apress titles may be purchased in bulk for academic, corporate, or promotional use. eBook versions and licenses are also available for most titles. For more information, reference our Print and eBook Bulk Sales web page at http://www.apress.com/bulk-sales.

Any source code or other supplementary material referenced by the author in this book is available to readers on GitHub (https://github.com/Apress). For more detailed information, please visit https://www.apress.com/gp/services/source-code.

Paper in this product is recyclable

Table of Contents

About the Author

Tasha Penwell is an AWS Educator and AWS Authorized Instructor, solutions architect, and an AWS Security and Identity Community Builder. In her career, she served as the Computer Science Program Manager for a community college in Ohio. Tasha has trained professionals on AWS, web development, and data analytics. She is the founder and educator of Bytes and Bits `www.bytesandbits.org`, an organization that provides computer science education in Ohio and West Virginia. Tasha is passionate about teaching and bridging knowledge gaps in the rural areas. Her goal is to help build rural communities by providing resources and instruction on areas ranging from basic computer skills to more advanced skills such as web development and cloud computing. Tasha lives in Ohio with her husband and she can be reached on LinkedIn at `https://www.linkedin.com/in/tashapenwell/`.

About the Technical Reviewer

Ravi Devarasetty is a seasoned cybersecurity professional specializing in multicloud security, especially AWS. With over 22 years of experience, he worked on numerous projects focused on securing cloud environments and implementing robust security measures in AWS. He holds both the solutions architect associate and security specialty certifications in AWS and has successfully designed and implemented security architectures for various types of organizations (technology, financial, manufacturing, pharmaceutical, etc.), ensuring compliance with industry standards such as CIS and NIST and protecting sensitive data. His expertise extends to areas such as identity and access management, data encryption, compliance, and vulnerability management/remediation. He also has a variety of IT experience such as embedded software development, network and security operations, and engineering. He holds a master's degree in computer engineering and a bachelor's degree in electronics and communications engineering.

In addition to his practical experience, he is passionate about raising awareness of AWS security best practices and empowering others to strengthen their cloud security posture. He reviewed this book on AWS Security to contribute to the knowledge-sharing community and help professionals navigate the complex landscape of cloud security. He continues to stay updated with the latest developments in the field, actively engaging in research and participating in industry conferences. His goal is to make cloud security accessible and understandable for businesses of all sizes, enabling them to leverage the benefits of AWS with confidence. In his spare time, he also mentors IT professionals and helps with their transition to cloud security.

ABOUT THE TECHNICAL REVIEWER

Ravi lives in the United States with his wife and two children. He loves to spend time with family after work and enjoys taking scenic walks and vacations. Ravi also practices Indian yoga, meditation, and pranayama on a regular basis. You can connect with him on LinkedIn at `www.linkedin.com/in/ravikiran123`.

CHAPTER 1

Why Do I Care About Security?

You have successfully migrated to the cloud – or maybe you have successfully launched your application into the cloud. Congratulations! That is a great achievement, and the value that the cloud provides is only going to help your business grow and improve your customer's experience, and you no longer have to worry about security.

Well…that is not completely right. The value proposition that the cloud brings to your business is improved agility and elasticity which can provide a better experience for your customers, but security is not something you can offset to AWS. While AWS provides exceptional security for its data centers, you are responsible for what you put in. That's a distinction between security of the cloud and security in the cloud, which we get into later on.

When I'm teaching principles from the AWS Security Pillar and the Shared Responsibility Model, I make a comparison of AWS and your home's security.

There are some default security features to your home. Examples of those can be door locks, window locks, and maybe a dog that will scare away those would-be intruders. You have decided that you would like to provide extra security for peace of mind by purchasing a security alarm and monitors to ensure that your family is protected, and if someone should try to break through default features, the security alarm will trigger a notification to your local law enforcement so they can come help.

© Tasha Penwell 2023
T. Penwell, *Beginning AWS Security*, https://doi.org/10.1007/978-1-4842-9681-3_1

You are set up and secure, but one day when you are running late for work, you forget to lock the door. An intruder breaks in, and when the alarm starts to sound, there is a brief moment of regret by the intruder — until they see that your alarm code is taped to the system to disable it, so no notification will be sent to the alarm company. You come home to find that you have been robbed, and your first thought is that the alarm company failed you because they did not send anyone to prevent the robbery.

But did it really? Think about it.

You didn't follow a basic security best practice – lock your door. You also left the code next to your alarm panel even though the security technicians specifically said to protect the code and not to keep it taped next to the panel.

This is an example of "shared responsibility." AWS provides resources and services to help you maintain your cloud security, but it is up to you to use them (lock the door) and follow best practices (don't tape the code next to the panel).

Now let's take this analogy to your application. When you deploy your application into the cloud, you are deploying them onto AWS's servers at their data centers around the world. AWS provides protection of their data centers at four layers: data, infrastructure, environmental, and perimeter. The application you deploy in those servers is protected physically, but it is up to you to protect the application and your customer's data on the networks. While the division of responsibility can change based on the services you use (managed or unmanaged), there is still a shared responsibility.

Protect What Is Valuable

You have deployed your application, and the data that you have collected is invaluable. Just as you want to protect your home so your family is safe and your property is not stolen, the data you collect can also play a role in your user's safety and ensure that their information is not stolen.

Following are three stories of organizations that had lapses in their security when using the AWS cloud.

Pegasus Airlines

In May 2022, Safety Detectives[1] security team discovered that Pegasus Airlines had left an AWS S3 (Simple Storage Service) bucket containing Pegasus Airlines' "Electronic Flight Bag" information without password protection. An Electronic Flight Bag (EFB) is a device that hosts applications that allow flight crews to perform a variety of functions that were previously completed using paper products and tools. EFBs[2] can contain everything from basic flight information or can be integrated with aircraft systems.

The PegasusEFB[3] itself is an EFB solution that provides full integration features and uses cloud technology. PegasusEFB is used by pilots for aircraft navigation, takeoff/landing, refueling, safety procedures, and other in-flight processes – information that should be private, but thanks to an open bucket, this information and crew members' personal identifiable information were not.

In addition, the leaky bucket also exposed EFB software's source code which contained plaintext passwords and secret keys that were not so secret.

Altogether, almost 23 million files were found on the bucket which totals to 6.5 TB of data. This type of exposure creates security concerns for every Pegasus passenger, crew member, and affiliated airlines that also use PegasusEFB.

---

[1] https://www.safetydetectives.com/news/pegasus-leak-report/.
[2] https://nbaa.org/aircraft-operations/communications-navigation-surveillance-cns/electronic-flight-bags/.
[3] https://pegasusefb.com/.

Capital One

As of 2022, the Federal Reserves[4] lists Capital One as the tenth largest consumer bank in the United States. When Capital One Financial Corporation announced that there was unauthorized access by an outside individual, they ranked seventh[5] in the United States. That was in 2019. Within three years, their ranking dropped from seventh to tenth.

In the July 29, 2019, press release[6] addressing this breach, one of the questions asked and answered was "Did this vulnerability arise because you operate in the cloud?" The answer was no – this type of vulnerability is not specific to the cloud. The elements involved are common to both cloud and on-premises data center environments. They further explain that "The speed with which we were able to diagnose and fix this vulnerability, and determine its impact, was enabled by our cloud operating model."

So what happened? According to the indictment[7] from July 29, 2019, Paige Thompson (a former Amazon software engineer) exploited a vulnerability in its firewall configuration that permitted commands to reach and be executed by that server. This vulnerability enabled access to buckets of data in Capital One's storage space at the Cloud Computing Company. *Note: AWS was not disclosed as the Cloud Computing Company in the indictment.* The attacker shared this vulnerability and commands to access customer data on GitHub which Capital One later confirmed was successful in obtaining private information of more than 700 buckets (folders) of data. Capital One states that the logs show a number of connections to Capital One's server from The Onion Router (TOR) exit nodes. Through this breach, the attacker was able to access data related to

---

[4] https://www.federalreserve.gov/releases/lbr/current/default.htm.

[5] https://www.federalreserve.gov/releases/lbr/20190630/default.htm.

[6] https://www.capitalone.com/about/newsroom/
capital-one-announces-data-security-incident/.

[7] https://www.justice.gov/usao-wdwa/press-release/file/1188626/download.

tens of millions of credit card applications. This includes approximately 120,000 social security numbers and approximately 77,000 bank account numbers. This data was only partially encrypted by Capital One.

With the magnitude of this data breach, there are articles with plenty of insights into what did happen and what Capital One could have done proactively. For the purpose of this book, we are going to focus on vulnerabilities like a misconfigured firewall, failure to monitor logs, failure to set up log notifications, failure to encrypt data, and not securing the S3 bucket accurately.

Accenture

In 2017, UpGuard[8] discovered four cloud storage buckets unsecured and publicly downloadable. This vulnerability exposed "secret API data, authentication credentials, certificates, decryption keys, customer information, and more data that could have been used to attack both Accenture and its clients." These four buckets were configured to be accessible to "anyone who entered the buckets' web address into their Internet browser." One bucket had information in a folder titled "Secure Store" that contained configuration files and plaintext documents with master access for Accenture's account with AWS KMS (Key Management Service) – exposing an unknown number of credentials. Another bucket exposed larger amounts of data that included credentials – some for Accenture clients. Some of these passwords were hashed, but there was still a collection of nearly 40,000 plaintext passwords in one of the database backups.

UpGuard further shared their insights that "Enterprises must be able to secure their data against exposures of this type." This could have been prevented, and this shows that organizations such as Accenture's (which have several number one rankings to their name) modern IT departments must be tenacious in proactively protecting their system.

---

[8] https://www.upguard.com/breaches/cloud-leak-accenture.

One thing I want to note is the distinction between responsibility for the attack and responsibility for the vulnerability – because those are not the same. With PegasusEFB and Accenture, cybersecurity firms appeared to find the vulnerability first and notified the companies of this vulnerability to allow them to properly update their infrastructure. In regard to Capital One's story, it is an example of an all-too-common scenario of someone finding the vulnerability left by business and taking advantage of it for personal gain, fame, or fortune.

Hackers

There are seven types of hackers[9] that businesses need to be aware of regardless of your infrastructure model:

1. Black Hat

    a. Known as "crackers"

    b. Cybercriminals who break security systems for malicious purposes

    c. Primary motivation is for financial gain

    d. Employed by foreign governments and organized criminal groups for espionage purposes

2. White Hat

    a. Known as "ethical hackers"

    b. Will help remove a virus or test a company's security defenses

3. Script Kiddie

    a. Known as a "skiddie"

---

[9] https://www.cybrary.it/blog/0p3n/types-of-hackers/.

    b. Lacks programming knowledge and IT security skills

    c. Uses existing security tools to launch cyberattacks

4. Gray Hat

    a. Doesn't penetrate IT systems for malicious intent

    b. Uses the same hacking techniques as Black Hat hackers to discover vulnerabilities and security flaws without the owner's permission

    c. Will report to the owner to fix but will request a small payment for their effort

    d. If the owner does not agree to pay, will publish the vulnerability online

    e. Still considered illegal because it did not have permission to find security flaws

5. Green Hat

    a. New to the hacking game

    b. Strive to master their skills (unlike skiddies)

6. Red Hat

    a. Hacker that targets Linux-based systems (many cloud computing systems use Linux)

    b. Target Black Hat hackers to cease their criminal activities or disclose their identity to the public

7. Blue Hat

    a. Script kiddie who takes revenge

    b. Newbies with no desire to learn

STOP and THINK

What type of hacker would you classify

- Paige Thompson

- Safety Detectives

- UpGuard

We just reviewed three real-world scenarios where AWS customers had a serious data exposure that could have impacted their individual customers' safety, security, and identity. While there are some debate and court cases on how much responsibility AWS should bear in these breaches, the status quo states that AWS provides the resources, training, and services, and the burden goes to the customers to implement them. The point of contention for many using the cloud is the ease of misconfiguration of the platform or assumptions on security in the cloud being offset to AWS's burden as they adopt more cloud computing resources. AWS does provide documentation to clarify the burdens, but nuances in types of services can make it a little more complicated than it may seem at first.

We've already mentioned the Shared Responsibility Model which helps distinguish responsibility. Tables 1-1 and 1-2 review some of the security services and resources AWS provides along with information if this is a paid service or a free service (yes, some of them are available for free – you just need to use them).

Table 1-1. *AWS security services and pricing*

AWS Service	Pricing*
AWS Trusted Advisor	Varies depending on AWS Plan
AWS Well-Architected Framework	No charge
AWS Well-Architected Framework Tool	No charge
AWS CloudTrail	Free tier and Paid tier
Amazon CloudWatch	Free tier and Paid tier
Amazon IAM	No charge

(continued)

Table 1-1. (*continued*)

AWS Service	Pricing*
AWS Config	Paid service
Amazon GuardDuty	Paid service
Amazon Detective	Paid service
AWS Network Firewall	Paid service
AWS Firewall Manager	Paid service
AWS Shield	Paid service
AWS WAF (web application firewall)	Paid service
AWS KMS	Paid service
AWS Security Hub	Paid service
AWS Inspector	Paid service
Amazon Macie	Paid service
Service Control Policies (used with AWS Organizations)	No charge
Amazon Security Lake	Paid service

Table 1-2. *AWS security resources and pricing*

AWS Service	Pricing*
Training (Skill Builder)	No charge
Training (AWS Educate)	No charge
Well-Architected Guidance	No charge
Well-Architected Lenses	No charge
Documentation	No charge

Services at no charge can include use of services that will receive charges.

The Well-Architected Framework

Now that you have some insights on how customers continue to have responsibilities to securing data, let's look at how AWS can help us do that. In Figure 1-1, you can see six pillars that AWS has developed that provide the foundation to help its customers make the best decision to secure their data and build a reliable, durable, and highly available environment.

Pillars of the Well-Architected Framework

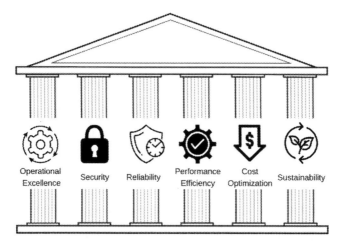

Figure 1-1. *AWS Well-Architected Framework*

Ultimately, most things in life are about trade-offs. Time, money, security, ease of use, and more are all things we make decisions on to trade for another. You are trading your time right now reading this book to improve your skills to build a secure AWS cloud architecture. While a general mentality of being a lifelong learner could be your motivation, you are also likely aware of the career benefits and increased compensation that come with your investment in your skills. You are trading the time that you could be spending doing something else – maybe cleaning your home, for example. For that, you could hire a housekeeper to come in once or twice a week, so you can spend your time improving your skills. Your housekeeper is trading their time away from their family and friends to earn money from you as they clean your home. You are again trading money for additional time to focus on your studies.

Just as you make decisions in your daily life, you need to make the same decisions for your cloud infrastructure. The Well-Architected Framework helps you understand these trade-offs so you can make the best decisions for your organization's needs. The Framework will help you design your cloud architecture to meet specific requirements on reliability, security, efficiency, and cost-effectiveness (uncontrolled costs have brought many a cloud architect down). AWS provides the tools, but just as we spoke about the home security example earlier, it's up to you to use them effectively. These six pillars are

1. Operational excellence

2. Security

3. Reliability

4. Performance efficiency

5. Cost optimization

6. Sustainability

Now that you understand that decisions on trade-offs will need to be made, let's review the Security Pillar in greater detail. The Security Pillar is designed to be used by individuals in roles like chief technology officers, chief information security officers, cloud architects, cloud developers, and operations team members. Even if your role does not require in-depth knowledge of how to build a secure cloud infrastructure, understanding the techniques, strategies, and trade-offs will make you stronger and more proactive in your architecture's security needs.

Security in the cloud is defined into six different areas:

1. Foundations

2. Identity and access management

3. Detection

4. Infrastructural protection

5. Data protection

6. Incident response

...and with seven different design principles:

1. Implement a strong identity foundation.

2. Enable traceability of who is doing what and when.

3. Apply security at all layers.

4. Automate security best practices.

5. Protect data in transit and at rest.

6. Keep people away from data.

7. Prepare for security events.

Shared Responsibility Model

One of the basic cornerstones of AWS security is based on the Shared Responsibility Model. This will be covered in more detail in a later chapter, but it is basically summed up as follows:

AWS is responsible for the security of the cloud.

Customer is responsible for security in the cloud.[10]

What does that mean? Review the diagram from AWS[11] shown in Figure 1-2.

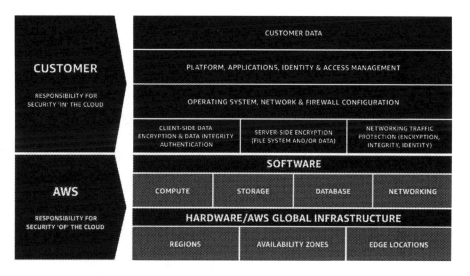

Figure 1-2. *Shared Responsibility Model*

Notice there are two sections – the Customer (security "in" the cloud) and AWS (security "of" the cloud). All cloud service providers have a similar model – this is not unique to AWS. The purpose is to help provide a clear distinction between responsibilities, so customers don't mistakenly think AWS is maintaining security in areas that is not their responsibility.

---

[10] https://aws.amazon.com/compliance/shared-responsibility-model/#:~:text=AWS%20responsibility%20%E2%80%9CSecurity%20of%20the,that%20run%20AWS%20Cloud%20services

[11] https://aws.amazon.com/compliance/shared-responsibility-model/

Consider the home security system analogy again. You have the top-of-the-line security system to protect your family residing in it. What would happen if you left the front door open – or a back door was left unlocked? An intruder could find their way in which would make your family vulnerable to the intruder. As we discussed earlier, that is not the security alarm company's fault because it's a reasonable measure of responsibility for you to keep your doors closed and locked.

Now instead of it being your home and home security system, it's your database or a web application that you have living in the cloud. AWS provides protection at four different layers to make up the security "of" the cloud. These layers are perimeter, infrastructure, data, and environmental,[12] but it's your responsibility to use services and best practices to protect the data living on the servers in AWS's data centers.

Before moving on, let's explore the four layers of security that AWS provides to maintain their part of the Shared Responsibility Model (remember, they are responsible for security "of" the cloud).

AWS's Layers of Security for Data Centers

Perimeter Layer: AWS restricts physical access to people who need to be at a data center location for a justified reason. To be approved to access these discrete data centers, an application must be processed with a valid business justification. Access is granted as needed for as long as needed and revoked once the work has been completed. Once access is granted, entry is monitored with security cameras and MFA (multifactor authentication) to limit to preapproved areas.

Infrastructure Layer: Maintaining the infrastructure of the hardware in the data centers is a responsibility of AWS. One of the benefits of using cloud computing models is that you no longer need to maintain the physical infrastructure or protection from hazards as you would in

---

[12] https://aws.amazon.com/compliance/data-center/data-centers/

on-premise solutions. AWS maintains the machines providing those servers (even serverless computing has a server) running diagnostics on machines, networks, and backup equipment to ensure they are working; maintenance is planned ahead so that customers can be made aware via the AWS Health Dashboard.[13]

Data Layer: Access to the data center does not mean access to the server rooms. Access to the data is limited and only granted after a review and approval process. Intrusion detection systems (IDS) are also in place to trigger alerts of identified threats or suspicious activity. Access points to the server rooms are fortified and require MFA for access and attempts of electronic intrusion by warning employees of any attempts to remove data. In the event a breach does occur, the server is automatically disabled.

Environmental Layer: AWS has geographic locations comprised of Regions, Availability Zones, Local Zones, Edge Locations, and other points of presence around the globe. Customers have the opportunity to select the locations for their services based on their specific needs. While redundancy and disaster recovery options are also the responsibility of the customer, AWS is proactive to prevent potential environmental threats. These threats can come in the form of natural disasters (hurricanes, floods, blizzards, earthquakes, etc.) or fire. Data centers are equipped with sensors and equipment to respond to threats.

Reviewing the preceding four layers as AWS's responsibility can help you understand what is meant by responsibility "of" the cloud. It can be best summarized that they are responsible for protecting their tangible property from attacks or threats.

The applications customers build or the data they input into the cloud is not the property of AWS. You can discontinue services, migrate your data elsewhere, and close out your accounts if you choose to. These are

---

[13] https://health.aws.amazon.com/health/status

examples of how the data you place in the cloud and the services you select are your responsibility. We will cover this and the challenges of aligning to the Shared Responsibility Model more in Chapter 2.

Earlier, we reviewed three different scenarios where a vulnerability in a company's cloud environment was found. Even though not all were exploited, it's still indicative that there is a need for additional training and understanding beyond reviewing the chart of who is responsible for what.

It Depends

One of the most frustrating and accurate answers to tech-related questions is "it depends." This is also true in terms of responsibility in cloud computing. Cloud service providers such as AWS provide a variety of options available to allow their customers to customize their infrastructure based on their needs and their accepted trade-offs. Areas of trade-offs can include development efforts, maintenance efforts, availability, control, performance, and usability. As of this writing, there are over 200 different service options with AWS, and they are still growing based on market demands and customer requests and feedback.

Let's look at a sample of options available – and thus the decisions to be made with the foundational categories: Compute, Networking, Storage, and Databases. These services can be found on the AWS Documentation[14] and are shown in Figure 1-3.

---

[14] https://docs.aws.amazon.com/

Compute	Storage
Amazon EC2	Amazon S3
AWS App Runner	AWS Backup
AWS Batch	Amazon EBS
AWS Elastic Beanstalk	Amazon EFS
Amazon EC2 Image Builder	AWS Elastic Disaster Recovery
AWS End-of-Support Migration Program (EMP) for Windows Server	Amazon FSx
AWS Lambda	Amazon S3 Glacier
Amazon Lightsail	AWS Snow Family
AWS Outposts	AWS Storage Gateway
AWS ParallelCluster	
AWS Serverless Application Model (AWS SAM)	
AWS Serverless Application Repository	
AWS Wavelength	

Figure 1-3. *AWS services for compute, storage, databases, networking, and content delivery*

Database	Networking & Content Delivery
Amazon Aurora	Amazon API Gateway
Amazon DocumentDB	AWS App Mesh
Amazon DynamoDB	AWS Cloud Map
Amazon ElastiCache	Amazon CloudFront
Amazon Keyspaces (for Apache Cassandra)	AWS Direct Connect
Amazon MemoryDB for Redis	Elastic Load Balancing
Amazon Neptune	AWS Global Accelerator
Amazon QLDB	AWS Private 5G
Amazon RDS	Amazon Route 53
Amazon Redshift	Amazon VPC
Amazon Timestream	AWS VPN

Figure 1-3. *(continued)*

As you can see, AWS provides a variety of options, and as a cloud professional, you need to identify what trade-offs are to be made.

In the vulnerability scenarios we reviewed earlier, one of the common services among them all was the unsecured data in AWS Simple Storage Service (S3).

S3

Simple Storage Service (S3) is one of AWS's most used services. It's an object storage service that provides a scalable and durable platform that can hold a large variety of media types and data for backup and recovery. It provides scalability, data availability, and performance.

Security with S3 is focused on protecting data. The CIA (confidentiality, integrity, and availability) triad (Figure 1-4) is a commonly used model to guide policies on data security and is applicable to the data stored in S3.

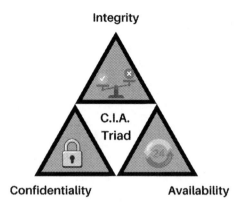

Figure 1-4. *Confidentiality, integrity, and availability (CIA) triad*

Referring to the Security Pillar in the Well-Architected Framework, the foundational practices that help design the security policies should be in place. Think of it as the blueprint before you begin building the infrastructure (this analogy works with the cloud or a physical building). Some foundational practices to take into consideration for S3 are the following:

1. **Data classification**: Data classification provides a way to categorize organizational data based on criticality and sensitivity in order to help you determine appropriate protection and retention controls.[15]

---

[15] https://docs.aws.amazon.com/wellarchitected/latest/security-pillar/data-classification.html

2. **Protecting data at rest**: Data at rest represents any data that persists in nonvolatile storage for any duration in your workload. Protecting your data at rest reduces the risk of unauthorized access, when encryption and appropriate access controls are implemented.[16]

3. **Protecting data in transit**: Data in transit is any data that is sent from one system to another. By providing the appropriate level of protection for your data in transit, you protect the confidentiality and integrity of your workload's data.[17]

With these foundational practices in mind, let's briefly review the vulnerabilities in the case studies of PegasusEFB, Capital One, and Accenture.

PegasusEFB

- Data stored in plaintext

- Open bucket containing personal identifiable information of crew members and customers among other sensitive information

Capital One

- Firewall misconfiguration for the virtual server enabled successful penetration.

- Penetration to the virtual server enabled access to S3 buckets.

---

[16] https://docs.aws.amazon.com/wellarchitected/latest/security-pillar/protecting-data-at-rest.html

[17] https://docs.aws.amazon.com/wellarchitected/latest/security-pillar/protecting-data-in-transit.html

Accenture

- Buckets exposing confidential information such as API data, authentication credentials, customer information, and more

- Plaintext documents containing the master access key for AWS's Key Management Service (KMS) which exposes credentials for malicious use

Fortunately, only one of the three examples had someone using the vulnerability for personal gain and/or fame. The other two were found by security firms that ethically reported the vulnerabilities to their owners.

What are some commonalities you see in the three examples?

1. S3 bucket vulnerabilities

2. Plaintext documents inside the buckets

Adopting the mindset that every misfortune can be an opportunity to learn from, what type of proactive approaches do you think these companies have going forward for their S3 buckets and the documents stored in it? Doing a better job of protecting it is obviously one answer, but how is that specifically done?

Let's start from the inside out with the **plaintext** documents. Plaintext documents are flat files that have content that is human readable. This can be in the format of a sentence, script, or even programming code. Even if you are not familiar with a particular language (communication or programming purposes), someone else will be able to read and interpret what is being shared in this unprotected document.

To add an additional layer of protection beyond the firewalls and MFA, storing the documents as ciphertext will provide an additional layer of protection. **Ciphertext** is text that has been encrypted and now displays a series of randomized letters and numbers which makes no sense to humans. This is done by using an encryption algorithm in a plaintext message that produces a ciphertext output. Authorized users can then decrypt this information by reversing this process to display the original plaintext.

> In January 2023, AWS announced that all data in S3 will be encrypted by default using SSE-S3.[18]

Now that we've discussed how to ensure documents are protected on their own, it's time to examine those S3 vulnerabilities.

Amazon S3 provides a variety of security features to consider into your security policies. Remember, your security is only as tough as you build it to be.

S3 Preventative Security Best Practices[19]

1. Ensure that your S3 bucket and policies are not publicly accessible.

   a. Use the correct policies.

   b. Do not make it publicly available.

      i. Use S3 block public access.

   c. Identify and review any S3 bucket policies that allow a wildcard identity in the "Principal" or "Action" parts of the policy statement.

   d. Identify and review any bucket access control lists that provide read, write, or full access to everyone.

---

[18] https://docs.aws.amazon.com/AmazonS3/latest/userguide/UsingEncryption.html

[19] https://docs.aws.amazon.com/AmazonS3/latest/userguide/security-best-practices.html#security-best-practices-detect

    e. Use AWS Trusted Advisor to inspect your S3 architecture.

    f. Use the ListBuckets API to scan all of your Amazon S3 buckets to determine whether the buckets have compliant access controls and configuration on the APIs: GetBucketAcl, GetBucketWebsite, and GetBucketPolicy.

    g. Consider using detective controls with AWS Config rules.

2.   Maintain the principle of least privilege when granting access via IAM.

3.   Use an IAM role to assign temporary credentials as needed instead of distributing long-term credentials.

4.   Encrypt your data at rest both on the server side and customer side.

5.   Enforce encryption of data when it's in transit.

6.   Enable versioning to be able to roll back to previous versions if data was compromised.

7.   Enable cross-region replication to provide higher availability to resource.

8.   Control access to the S3 buckets by limiting traffic from specific Virtual Private Cloud (VPC) endpoints.

Once security is implemented, monitoring is an important follow-up and repeated step. In Accenture and PegasusEFB, only a limited portion of its architecture was vulnerable. Systems are built by people, and with personnel changes, insufficient training, or simple accidental oversight, misconfigurations do happen. By monitoring and auditing, you are setting yourself up for successful security measures and meeting any needed compliance requirements.

S3 Monitoring and Auditing

1. Identify and audit all your S3 buckets.

2. Use key:value tags to identify sensitive information.

3. Use the monitoring tools!

    a. CloudWatch

    b. CloudTrail

4. Use AWS Config to review changes in configurations and relationships between resources, investigate configuration histories, and determine overall compliance.

5. Use Amazon Macie to identify any sensitive data in your bucket.

6. Check Trusted Advisor for warnings on "open access permissions."

Despite best efforts and proper training, misconfigurations are still a reality. Accidental or intentional, misconfigurations can lead to breaches that can have dire impacts to an organization's ability to maintain the security of confidential data and maintain compliance to service-level agreements. One of the major benefits of using cloud technologies is the ability to automate when configurations are no longer meeting organizations' standards and policies. Corrective tools allow organizations to be reactive when proactive security measures failed.

S3 Corrective Tools

S3 monitoring and auditing activities use AWS Config to review changes in configuration and resources to determine overall compliance. Config can be used with AWS Systems Manager and runbooks to ensure that configurations are in compliance. Using AWS Systems Manager Automation, the AWS customer can use automation to configure and manage AWS resources.

If a resource becomes noncompliant based on configuration rules applied to it, this vulnerability can be rectified in minutes using runbooks provided by AWS or custom rules to suit specific organizational needs.

An example of an AWS Config managed rule is the s3-bucket-public-read-prohibited. In the managed rule, an organization's S3 bucket will deny attempts to be read by the general public. It checks for the Block Public Access settings, the bucket policy, and the bucket access control list (ACL).

If the following items are true, then the rule is considered compliant:

- Block Public Access setting restricts public policies, or the bucket policy does not allow public read access.

- Block Public Access setting restricts public ACLs, or the bucket ACL does not allow public read access.

A trigger is activated if the Block Public Access settings are changed or on periodic checks specified.

Well-Architected Framework Tools

We've talked about the Well-Architected Framework and the suggestions and directions it provides to help maintain a secure architecture, but that's not all it provides. Despite the appearance of a clear line of division on responsibilities in the Shared Responsibility Model, implementing it is less than clear, and the answer of "security of" or "security in" can revert back to "it depends." This is, in large part, due to the different categories of services that cloud service providers like AWS provide.

The three types of services can be categorized as

1.   Infrastructure as a Service (IaaS)

2.   Platform as a Service (PaaS)

3.   Software as a Service (SaaS)

The difference in the type of service plays a large role in where the line falls on between AWS and the customer in terms of responsibility.

With IaaS services like Elastic Compute Cloud (EC2), the customer has granular levels of control over the architecture, which means they also carry the most responsibility in maintaining the security.

PaaS services such as Relational Database Service (RDS) allow AWS to carry more of the responsibility for the trade-off of less granular control by the customer. (Remember, there's a trade-off to everything.)

SaaS services such as CloudWatch are fully under the umbrella of AWS to maintain and keep secure and require little from the customer.

The AWS Well-Architected Tool[20] (AWS WA Tool) is a service to provide a process to measure your AWS architecture against best practices.

Cloud, On-premise, or Hybrid

In addition to the flexibility in types of service, customers also have the opportunity to decide the type of architecture – and their own set of security questions to consider for that.

Cloud Infrastructure: All services are 100% in the cloud. This can include selecting one single cloud provider or choosing to adopt a multicloud approach by using more than one cloud service provider.

On-premise: The organization chooses to maintain services on-premise and utilize the cloud resources to support some business practices by connecting to AWS public endpoints.

---

[20] https://docs.aws.amazon.com/wellarchitected/latest/userguide/intro.html.

Hybrid: A hybrid service uses a combination of cloud and on-premise features and tactics.

The reasons that a customer may have to select one type of architecture over another can be based on a variety of factors from trust, costs, fear, skill, etc. Regardless of the reason, this is yet another decision that cloud professionals must face as they decide if/when to adopt cloud computing for their IT needs.

Traditional Architecture

A traditional IT infrastructure requires large upfront capital expenditures. It is made up of hardware and software components, such as servers, networking hardware, desktop computers, software for business needs that can include HR, Customer Management Systems (CMS), Enterprise Resource Planning (ERP), etc., and the facilities to maintain and protect these machines.

Remember, AWS does this as well for their own data centers. By using cloud service providers, we are offsetting those costs and headaches to AWS and the costs of their services depending on what resources we use.

Cloud Architecture

In a cloud computing IT infrastructure, no capital expenditures are needed. Expenses are based on services used during operations. These are referred to as variable or operational expenses. Cloud service providers like AWS provide their customers access to the infrastructure via the Internet. These services include foundational services discussed earlier like computing, networking, storage, and databases. Many cloud service providers have grown beyond those four types of services as technology continues to advance and there is a demand on access to resources such as IoT software, quantum computing, artificial intelligence, and more. Hypervisor technology is used to connect the cloud servers to their customers.

Prescriptive Guidance

In this chapter, you learned about some organizations whose data was left vulnerable and failed to follow best practices. Whether due to lack of skill, guidance, or just old-fashioned human error is difficult to say. What is not difficult to say is there are a lot of moving pieces in the cloud, and that is largely due to its microservice model that allows the customers to customize their environment based on their infrastructure needs.

AWS has a variety of microservices for security controls alone, so they have developed a Prescriptive Guidance[21] that can be used to help their customers strategize and accelerate cloud migration and embrace optimization and modernization. The guides and patterns were developed by AWS technology experts and AWS partners to help customers make the best choices for their business and security needs.

The Prescriptive Guidance provides three types of security controls based on three periods of time security professionals will find themselves in:

1. Before the attack (Preventative)

2. During the attack (Detective)

3. After the attack (Responsive)

The Preventative Controls are designed to prevent an attack or event from occurring. Preventative Controls are where the phrase "the best defense is a good offense" comes to mind. You don't have to worry about the other team scoring if they never get the ball. In Table 1-3 are a list of AWS services and a short description of how they can provide preventative measures.

---

[21] https://docs.aws.amazon.com/prescriptive-guidance/latest/aws-security-controls/security-control-types.html

Table 1-3. *AWS services and how they are used for preventative measures*

AWS Service	Preventative Measures
AWS Service Control Policies	• SCPs define the maximum available permissions for member accounts in an AWS Organization. They can be used to define and enforce allowable permissions for IAM users or roles in an Organization's member account • Can also be used to define maximum permission on a Region by Region basis
AWS Identity and Access Management	• IAM is used to set the maximum permission for an identity-based policy to users, roles, groups, and services

The Detective Controls are designed to detect, log, and create an alert after an event has taken place. These are the guardrails at the second line of defense. This is when the other team has the ball, and you are working hard to get it back from them before they score. At this stage, you have been notified of a security event that made it past the offensive line. If you have ever watched an (American) football game, you know it is only a matter of time before that quarterback gets sacked. In Table 1-4 are a list of AWS services and a short description of how they can provide detective measures.

Table 1-4. *AWS services and how they are used for detective*
measures

AWS Service	Detective Measures
Amazon GuardDuty	• Uses threat intelligence, machine learning, and anomaly detection techniques • Monitors log sources for malicious activity • Provides dashboard with real-time health status updates
AWS Security Hub	• Checks for adherence to best practices, aggregates alerts to one dashboard • Enables automated remediation • Receives findings from GuardDuty to provide a central repository of suspicious activity
Amazon Macie	• Fully managed data security and data privacy service • Uses machine learning and pattern matching to discover and protect sensitive data • Uses managed and custom data identifiers • Integrates with EventBridge to send findings to Security Hub
AWS Config	• Audits and records compliance of AWS resources • Identifies AWS services in use and creates a full inventory of resources with configuration details of each • Records and provides a notification if there are any configuration changes
AWS Trusted Advisor	• Can be used as a service for detective controls • Available on all service plans with additional features for Business and Enterprise service plans • Performs checks to identify areas that can be optimized to improve security
Amazon Inspector	• Automated vulnerability management service • Scans workloads continuously for unintended exposure or vulnerabilities

The Responsive Controls are designed to support and foster remediation of these attacks and events. Responsive Controls are focused on how you recover and learn from a security attack or event. To finish up on the sports analogy, this is how you react after the other team scores a touchdown (or wins the entire game). There are lessons to be learned on how to improve completed yards, protecting the quarterback, and such. This is where you learn how to improve your preventive measures. In Table 1-5 are a list of AWS services and a short description of how they can provide responsive measures.

Table 1-5. *AWS services and how they are used for responsive measures*

AWS Service	Responsive Measures
AWS Config	• Uses rules to evaluate AWS resources and remediate noncompliant resources • Uses Systems Manager Automation to define the actions to perform on resources that AWS Config determines to be noncompliant
AWS Security Hub	• Automatically sends new findings and updates of existing findings to EventBridge • Custom actions can be created to send specified findings and insight results to EventBridge
Amazon Macie	• Fully managed data security and data privacy service • Uses machine learning and pattern matching to discover and protect sensitive data • Uses managed and custom data identifiers • Integrates with EventBridge to send findings to Security Hub
AWS Systems Manager	• Creates runbooks for common types of attacks

Summary

In this chapter, you learned that just because you've decided to offset infrastructure responsibility to AWS does not mean you've offset security. Vulnerabilities will continue to exist, and the Shared Responsibility Model with cloud service providers state that the customer has control (and thus responsibility) of maintaining their data's confidentiality, integrity, and availability. AWS provides a series of tools with a framework to help cloud architects decide what trade-offs are necessary and how the shift of responsibility changes based on decisions made.

CHAPTER 2

Who Is Responsible Again?

In this chapter, we go deeper into the shared responsibilities that AWS and the customer share. Ultimately, a big factor that determines responsibility is the type of resource – IaaS, PaaS, or SaaS. AWS's Shared Responsibility Model does not provide a clear distinction of responsibilities, but there is in fact a distinction – which is why I introduce Microsoft's Azure Shared Responsibility Model in my classes. Azure's model provides a clearer picture of distinction that can help with understanding. This chapter also covers changing technologies that have required the DIE (distributed, immutable, and ephemeral) model to complement the CIA triad that many cybersecurity principles are built upon. AWS goes through great efforts to protect its infrastructure around the world. Resources like the Well-Architected Framework and IAM are available to help customers build a secure environment.

© Tasha Penwell 2023
T. Penwell, *Beginning AWS Security*, https://doi.org/10.1007/978-1-4842-9681-3_2

Detailed Overview of the Shared Responsibility Model

In the previous chapter, you were introduced to the Shared Responsibility Model. Understanding this model is instrumental in developing a secure cloud infrastructure. As shown in Figure 2-1, it delineates the responsibilities by layers, but there are some areas of "it depends" where the division of responsibility may not be clear.

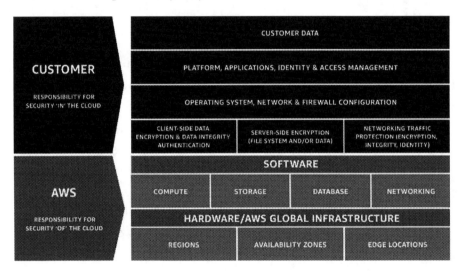

Figure 2-1. *The AWS Shared Responsibility Model*

The AWS Shared Responsibility Model is separated into two distinct areas of responsibility – the Customer and AWS. With a wide variety of services that include both managed and unmanaged services, it's essential to know that the division may not always be based on the *type* of services you are using – but on *what* specific resources you are using.[1] As you

---

[1] An AWS resource is an entity you can work with. An AWS service is what that resource does. For example, IAM is a resource that provides the service of managing user access.

probably already know, AWS isn't the only cloud service provider that organizations can adopt. Microsoft Azure is also a popular cloud service provider. AWS was launched in 2006,[2] which means it has a few years over Microsoft Azure as a cloud service provider which was launched in 2010. However, Microsoft has been in the computing space far longer than Amazon. When teaching about AWS Cloud Security and the Shared Responsibility Model, I like to also introduce Azure's diagram of the Shared Responsibility Model as shown in Figure 2-2.

Notice in Azure's Shared Responsibility Model in Figure 2-2 the headings of SaaS, PaaS, IaaS, and On-prem. These represent some options that customers can use when deploying into the cloud. On the far right, you see On-prem which represents organizations that continue to use on-premise models with their technology infrastructure being maintained internally on-site without using a public cloud service provider.

Three Types of Service Models

Cloud service providers (CSPs) provide three different types of service models – Infrastructure as a Service (IaaS), Platform as a Service (PaaS), and Software as a Service (SaaS). CSPs provide different types of resources for each service category to provide their customers the flexibility and support they need to meet their organizational goals, compliance needs, and overall objectives when deciding to migrate to the cloud.

IaaS services provide the infrastructure (i.e., servers, storage devices, etc.) to their customers, and the customers are responsible for developing the environment and security measures needed at a granular level. This means that more responsibility falls on the shoulders of the customer and

---

[2] https://aws.amazon.com/about-aws/

less on the CSP. This level of responsibility is often due to additional needs by an organization to maintain granular control over the services and how they are hosted (multitenancy or single tenancy, for example).

PaaS services are largely classified as managed services. Managed services allow the customer to focus more on their business services and products by offsetting the responsibility of maintaining security at the granular level to the CSP instead of self-managing as is done with IaaS service models.

SaaS services require little effort and maintenance from the customers. Think of the last time you signed up for a new email account. You created the account by filling in the required information, and almost instantly it was done. You have little control over how your email is configured in the backend and where the data is stored. There are setting options, of course, but they provide a surface level of protection instead of a more granular level. Most likely, you are okay with this level of access and control over your email because all you want to do is use it and accept that the service provider (Google, Microsoft, etc.) will provide the necessary protection of services beyond your settings.

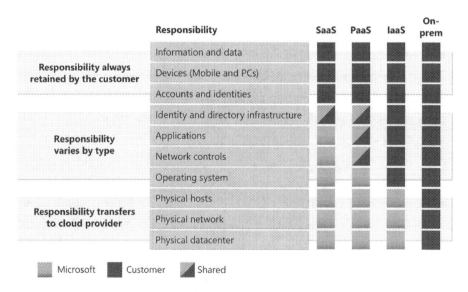

Figure 2-2. *Microsoft Azure's Shared Responsibility Model*

Take a moment and review the two diagrams side by side. Notice that there's a third level of "Responsibility varies by type" in the Azure model with a breakdown between Software as a Service (SaaS), Platform as a Service (PaaS), Infrastructure as a Service (IaaS), and On-premise (On-prem). While this is not as apparent in the AWS Shared Responsibility Model, it is also true for them.

The Shared Responsibility Model is often referred to as a model to identify areas of responsibility for security. AWS states *Security and Compliance is a shared responsibility between AWS and the customer. This shared model can help relieve the customer's operational burden as AWS operates, manages, and controls the components from the host operating system and virtualization layer down to the physical security of the facilities in which the service operates.*[3] It is certainly a foundation for building a secure cloud environment and a reference to use to build a platform that meets your availability needs.

To show an example of this, I'm going to compare what a company would need to consider in terms of security and availability for a MySQL database. There are two different ways that this can be done using AWS services. One is to build the database using an EC2 virtual machine. Elastic Compute Cloud (EC2) is an IaaS service. The other service to consider is Relational Database Service (Amazon RDS). RDS is one of the fully managed services with AWS and is a PaaS. Table 2-1 provides a comparison of the two services.

---

[3] https://aws.amazon.com/compliance/shared-responsibility-model/

Table 2-1. *Comparing two options for creating a database on AWS*

IaaS (EC2) Customer Responsibilities	PaaS (RDS) Customer Responsibilities
All necessary security configurations	Managing and encrypting data
All necessary security management	Classifying their assets
Managing, updating, and patching guest OS	Managing access permissions
Any application software or utilities installed by the customer onto the instance	
Configuration of the security group	

In general, if a customer selects an IaaS model, they are responsible for guest operating systems (including updates and patches) and the configuration of virtual firewalls (security groups and network access control lists).

According to AWS's documentation on AWS Cloud Security,[4] AWS is responsible for protecting the infrastructure that runs all the services. Remember, as you learned from Chapter 1, AWS maintains the high security of its data centers. This infrastructure includes the hardware, software, networking, and facilities that run AWS cloud services. Remember, the simplest explanation of the cloud is it's "someone else's computer" that we access using the Internet.

In terms of customers' responsibility, it's everything they select to use or put in their cloud environment – hence, "security in the cloud." The AWS Cloud Security documentation states that the customer's responsibility is determined by the AWS cloud service that the customer selects (i.e., EC2 vs. RDS). The service selected is what determines the amount of configuration work the customer must perform to maintain security and provide expected availability to their end users.

---

[4] https://aws.amazon.com/compliance/shared-responsibility-model/

Take a moment to look at the two responsibility models (AWS and Azure) introduced earlier in this chapter. No distinction is apparent in the AWS model, but Azure does provide some distinction, which is why I also use this diagram in my classes. In the Azure diagram, you can see that IaaS services are completely under the responsibility of the customer (which is also true for AWS), whereas under PaaS services' responsibility can be either AWS or the customer. Using a competitor's diagram is not a reliable way to base all your cloud infrastructure decisions, but it does provide a benefit to help understand the nuances of responsibility.

While the AWS Shared Responsibility Model diagram doesn't state it as clearly as Azure's diagram, the documentation does speak on shared controls. These are the controls that apply to both the infrastructure and customer layers but have different perspectives. Under the shared controls, AWS provides the requirements for the infrastructure, and the customer must provide their own control implementation within the use of AWS services. Table 2-2 shows some of the individual responsibilities between AWS and the customer.

Table 2-2. *Individual responsibilities between AWS and the customer*

AWS Responsibility	Customer Responsibility
Patching and fixing flaws within the infrastructure	Patching guest OS and applications
Maintaining configuration of infrastructure devices	Configuring own guest OS, databases, and applications
AWS provides training to their own employees	Customers are responsible for providing training to their own employees using resources like Skill Builder and AWS Training events

Trade-Offs

Most things in life are about trade-offs. In Figure 2-3, you see how decisions are made everyday about trade-offs. You trade 8+ hours of your day to earn a wage that can support you and your family. You're trading time for money. If you have a long commute (or maybe even a short one), you may decide to grab breakfast or dinner from a local restaurant to save you time in buying groceries, preparing food, and any cleanup afterward. To save on that time, you spend money to buy prepared meals at a restaurant. By buying prepared meals at a restaurant, you have no control over the food preparation or ingredients used. If you have a sensitive food allergy, you may be at the mercy of the restaurant following proper procedures and following specific order requests. You trade the control of your meal to have someone else make it. You could decide to regain control again by preparing your own meals, but then you have to trade something to give yourself more time to purchase groceries, prepare your meal, and clean up.

Earning an income takes time away from other activities - just as grocery shopping, meal prep, and clean-up. You may rely more on restaurants to prepare your meal where you have no control over how your meal was prepared.

Reducing your working hours, reduces your income. Less working hours means more time for other things like grocery shopping, meal preparation, and clean-up.

Figure 2-3. *You make trade-offs every day when deciding where to spend your time*

This scenario could go on, but, hopefully, you get the idea that there are trade-offs in every decision you make. These trade-offs are usually centered around time, money, and/or control. As you can see in Figure 2-4, the same is true in regards to how you build your cloud infrastructure. Cloud service providers such as AWS provide a wide variety of resources and services that you can use to maintain a secure architecture.

Using IaaS model provides the customer complete control over the management and updates needed for their environment. This requires the customer to spend more time and resources to support the environment needs.

| Resources are spent on environment support and not on business needs | Time is spent on environment support and not on business needs | More control of environment |

Using PaaS model allows the customer to use resources that are managed by AWS. This allows the customer more time to focus on their business and not the environment it's built on.

| More resource to be used for business | More time to focus on business | Less control of environment |

Figure 2-4. *Cloud customers must decide where they want to spend their time and resources – supporting the business or the environment it is built on*

Let's spend some time reviewing one of the foundational principles of cybersecurity – the CIA triad. The CIA triad represents principles about maintaining data confidentiality, integrity, and availability.

Confidentiality: In Chapter 1, you read about the Capital One Data Breach and how the confidentiality of personally identifiable information was not maintained properly and the attacker was able to penetrate the firewalls, access the unencrypted data, and exfiltrate the data by running commands to copy the data from the S3 bucket. Confidentiality was not maintained by prevention of access and then by keeping some of the data in plaintext format instead of ciphertext. A trade-off a company may need to decide upon in terms of confidentiality is ensuring data is protected and not inhibiting the use of data for the organization's objectives. According to the Capital One press release[5] dated July 29, 2019:

> *The largest category of information accessed was information on consumers and small businesses as of the time they applied for one of our credit card products from 2005 through early 2019. This information included personal information Capital One routinely collects at the time it receives credit card applications, including names, addresses, zip codes/postal codes, phone numbers, email addresses, dates of birth, and self-reported income. Beyond the credit card application data, the individual also obtained portions of credit card customer data, including*
>
> *Customer status data, e.g., credit scores, credit limits, balances, payment history, and contact information*
> *Fragments of transaction data from a total of 23 days during 2016, 2017 and 2018*
> *No bank account numbers or Social Security numbers were compromised, other than:*
>
> - *About 140,000 Social Security numbers of our credit card customers*
>
> - *About 80,000 linked bank account numbers of our secured credit card customers*

As you can see, confidential information was made vulnerable to unauthorized individuals. Malicious use of this data can impact a person's credit which, in turn, could impact their ability to apply for credit cards and loans, affect their insurance rates, and maybe even some job opportunities.

---

[5] www.capitalone.com/about/newsroom/capital-one-announces-data-security-incident/

Integrity: The integrity principles focus on ensuring that the data being used is correct and has not been altered. In the Capital One Data Breach, it's not apparent that any integrity of the data was at risk. While the attacker did extract the data, it does not appear that she changed the data such as altering the credit scores, changing social security numbers, annual income, etc. Integrity focuses on whether the data being used is accurate and has not been altered without authorization.

Availability: Don't forget to cover your "A." Data has little use if it's not available to be used when needed. The Shared Responsibility Model is often used as a reference to who is responsible for security measures in the cloud, but I also use it as a reference to who is responsible for ensuring the availability of resources in the cloud. An organization should have in its possession a Business Continuity Plan (BCP) and a Disaster Recovery Plan (DRP). In these plans, a Recovery Time Objective (RTO) and a Recovery Point Objective (RPO) should be established (Figure 2-5). The RTO states the acceptable amount of time that systems or data can be unavailable. This varies for different industries. Some industries like banking, healthcare, etc., require immediate availability of data. Other industries such as social media platforms, gaming applications, etc., can handle a longer RTO. Similarly, the RPO is also dependent upon the industry. The RPO designates an acceptable amount of data that can be lost. Another way of thinking about this is how often you should make backups to your data. The RPO is the point in time that you last backed up your data. If it's done on a daily basis, your RPO is 24 hours.

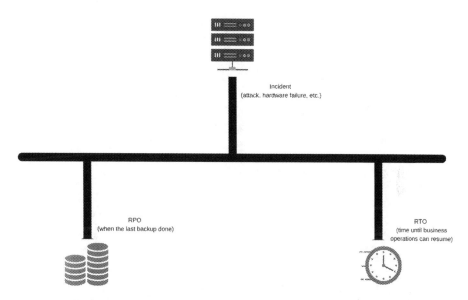

Figure 2-5. *Establishing an RPO and RTO is an important part of your DRP*

To put it in perspective, look at Figure 2-6 and think of your local bank. You made a deposit into your bank account at 9 am, but at 12 pm there was a cyberattack on the bank or a hardware failure. What would you want their RPO to be? Would 24 hours be sufficient? Of course not! It is unlikely that the backup happened between 9 am and 12 pm. You would expect your bank to have a more redundant system where data is replicated elsewhere away from the attack or hardware failure.

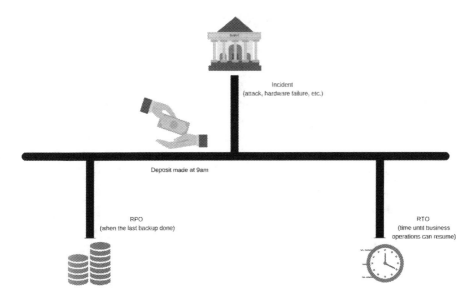

Figure 2-6. *An RPO of 24 hours can lose data about your deposit*

Take this same scenario and apply it to an online game or a social media platform. Would 24 hours be an acceptable RPO? Yes, it could be. While it could be an annoyance for some consumers to lose data like game scores, posts, photos, etc., it does not have the same catastrophic level that a banking institution would face.

How Does the CIA Triad Impact Trade-Offs?

Confidentiality: For data to be useful, it needs to be accessible to the proper individuals. It can be time-consuming to identify and manage which users in your organization should have access to data. To help identify this, the principle of least privilege (PoLP) is used to help enforce that only the users who need access to perform their job function have access. This defines "who can do what and where they can do it." This prevents all users from having the same types of access and instead applies specific actions at a granular level using Identity and Access Management (IAM) policies.

Integrity: For data to be useful, it also needs to be correct. Access logs can be used for audits and ensuring that data integrity is maintained. In general, most data is not static. It needs to be updated to reflect changes (i.e., bank account balance, inventory, etc.) as appropriate, but the individuals or methods to make these changes must be limited to align with the principle of least privilege. Auditing logs (such as CloudTrail logs) regularly in addition to ensuring that access to data is limited to a user's needs can enforce the integrity of data.

Availability: As I stated earlier, for data to be useful it needs to be available when it's needed. Once an RTO and RPO have been established, an organization needs to make decisions to build the infrastructure to support those recovery time and recovery point goals. The trade-off on this is money. To have a short RTO time, an infrastructure with replicated data needs to be on standby to be ready to provide services should the primary system fail. Similarly, if the RPO needs to be seconds, data needs to be replicated synchronously to another storage service. Having a system on standby and storage to replicate your primary storage needs to be built into your budget.

Before moving on, it's worth noting that the CIA triad was developed prior to cloud technologies being as widely adopted as they are today. Some of the changes and benefits of using the cloud vs. the traditional IT model are that the cloud is highly configurable. Within minutes, it provides a wide variety of resources and services that make a flexible, microservice-based architecture as opposed to a large, monolithic architecture. Services like AWS Organizations can create a centralized and consolidated way to manage multiple accounts and take advantage of economies of scale. With this great power and flexibility comes great responsibility and auditing. A microservice model and programmatic access can make configuration errors more prone. According to Gartner, the cloud user, not the cloud service provider, is responsible for security misconfigurations that can leave the architecture vulnerable to attack[6] (remember Capital One failed to encrypt all the data stored in S3 buckets).

With this changing landscape, it's worth diving into new design principles and their relationship with the CIA triad. These new design principles are distributed, immutable, and ephemeral (DIE).[7] These principles address some of the main challenges faced in maintaining a secure network. At the third Annual National Cybersecurity Summit, Sounil Yu shared how the DIE model (Figure 2-7) can counter the need for the CIA triad.[8]

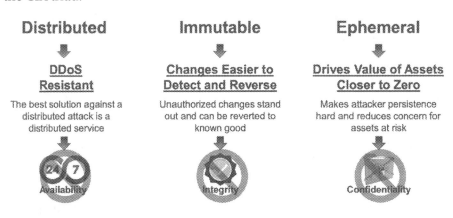

Figure 2-7. *DIE model*

Distributed: Availability can be impacted by data or servers not being available to respond to requests. A popular example of this is a DDoS attack. In traditional infrastructure, it would be difficult to combat this as server capacity is limited and the acquisition of new servers and storage media would be costly and time-consuming. AWS allows customers to build their infrastructure to scale. According to Yu, the best solution

---

[6] www.gartner.com/smarterwithgartner/is-the-cloud-secure
[7] https://pages.awscloud.com/rs/112-TZM-766/images/Protecting_sensitive_assets_AWS_Marketplace_Sounil_Yu_whitepaper.pdf
[8] www.cisa.gov/sites/default/files/publications/Daily_Keynote_with_Sounil_Yu_508pobs.pdf

to be DDoS resistant and ensure the "Availability" is not impacted is to build a distributed architecture. This can be done by using a Multi-AZ or Multi-Region approach and using Auto-Scaling Groups and Elastic Load Balancing to distribute the traffic to healthy endpoints. The idea is simple – if something is distributed, one source can go down without limiting overall availability.

Immutable: Immutable counters the Integrity component in the CIA triad. As you know, integrity focuses on the data being accurate and not being subject to unauthorized changes. If the data is immutable, any attempted unauthorized changes would stand out and can be reverted to the last known good data. The idea is that if something is immutable, it cannot be changed so integrity is in place.

Ephemeral: When I first begin learning about the cloud, I saw this word several times and had to look up the definition. I'll save you that trouble – it's a $10 word for temporary. Why couldn't they just say "temporary"? I don't know. That's a question for AWS. Ephemeral counters the Confidentiality component of the CIA triad by using services with short life spans like AWS Lambda, EC2 Instance Store, AWS IAM, and Security Token Service (STS). These resources are either natively temporary or can be made temporary by design and align with best practices. The idea is if something is ephemeral, it can make attacker persistence hard and reduce the concern for confidentiality.

While some could argue that the DIE triad replaces the CIA triad, I would disagree. With over 200 resources available on AWS, understanding and implementing best practices from both the CIA triad and DIE triad can help build a more secure architecture.

Review of AWS's Security Precautions (Security of the Cloud)

Let's review AWS's portion of responsibility in the Shared Responsibility Model. As we have already stated, AWS is responsible for the "security of the cloud." Let's explore that. As you know, AWS's network is comprised of Regions, Availability Zones, Edge Locations, and Local Zones. Within these Availability Zones, Edge Locations, and Local Zones reside data centers. These data centers and the computing hardware inside it are the responsibility of AWS. They have the responsibility "of" ownership – hence the security "of" the cloud. This responsibility can be divided into four layers: the perimeter layer, the infrastructure layer, the data layer, and the environmental layer.[9]

Perimeter Layer: Have you ever entered a secured facility? I used to live on a military base (Ft. Sill, Oklahoma), and to enter the base, you had to drive by armed military personnel and show your military ID verifying you were either military, a dependent, or had access otherwise. If not, you were required to leave the post. To make a purchase at the grocery or department stores on a post or use the healthcare facilities, you had to confirm you were military or a dependent by showing your military ID card. Other types of ID such as driver's licenses would not suffice because they did not show your status and ability to access services reserved for the military and families. AWS applies the same type of scrutiny to access its data centers. Security measures applied at the perimeter include the following:

- **Access is scrutinized.** Only personnel who have a business reason for being on-site are permitted. This access is monitored and reviewed regularly to ensure that access is still needed, and once work is completed, access is immediately revoked.

---

[9] https://aws.amazon.com/compliance/data-center/data-centers/

- **Access is monitored with security cameras.**
  Visitors are provided with badges that limit access to
  preapproved areas.

- **Data center personnel are also scrutinized.** The
  principle of least privilege is enforced for personnel
  to ensure that employees' access is limited to their job
  functions.

Infrastructure Layer: One of the benefits of using cloud technologies
is that environmental concerns such as space, HVAC, fire suppression, etc.,
are delegated to the cloud service provider. Security at the infrastructure
layer includes the following:

1) **Equipment maintenance**: AWS runs diagnostics on
   machines, networks, and backup systems to ensure
   they are operable and updated as needed.

2) **Emergency-ready backup equipment**: Electrical
   power systems are designed to be redundant, so a
   power outage can be recovered by using generators.

Data Layer: Tim Berners-Lee, the inventor of the World Wide Web,
once said that "Data is a precious thing and will last longer than the
systems themselves." Some would say that data is the new gold, and I
completely agree with that statement. I explain to my students that Data =
Information, Information = Knowledge, and Knowledge = Power. That is
why AWS considers the data layer the most critical layer to secure within
its data centers. It is the only area that holds customer data. Security at the
data layer includes the following:

1) **Technology and people**: Regular reviews of
   individuals who have access and intrusion detection
   systems are in place to monitor and trigger alerts for
   identified threats or suspicious activity.

2) **Preventing physical and electronic intrusion**: Access points require MFA to enter the server rooms. AWS servers are also equipped to warn employees of any attempts to remove data and automatically disable the server.

3) **Servers and media**: Media storage devices used to store customer data are considered critical and treated as such throughout their lifecycle. AWS has specific standards on the installation, service, and destroying them when they have reached end of life.

4) **Third-party auditors**: AWS is audited by auditors to ensure they are meeting more than 2600 requirements throughout the year.

Environmental Layer: Data centers have to go somewhere. Their location is largely based on environmental factors in an area that can support the demand for resources that the data centers will require. Security at the environmental layer focuses on the following:

1) **Preparing for natural disasters**: While AWS takes great care in selecting its data center locations, they are not making any more land, so AWS takes care in planning and preparing for natural disasters. This includes responsive equipment and automatic sensors that can detect a threat such as water or fire.

2) **Multiple Availability Zones**: The global infrastructure is made up of Regions and Availability Zones. As of 2022, there are 30 Regions and 96 Availability Zones (AZ) across the world. Each AZ consists of one or more data centers that are physically separate with redundant power and networking. *Note: It is up to the customer to*

take advantage of Multi-AZ and Multi-Region deployments. This is a perfect example of AWS providing it, but the customer needs to use it.

3) **AWS Business Continuity Plan**: The AWS BCP provides outlined processes to help prevent and mitigate disruptions due to natural disasters. AWS tests the BCP in different scenarios to ensure that personnel and processes are in place to rebound quickly.

As you can see, AWS goes to great lengths not only to ensure their property – the data centers and infrastructure itself – is secure from unauthorized access but to ensure that availability meets service-level agreements. This is the "security of the cloud." What the customer puts into it is another matter and where the Well-Architected Framework comes in.

Align How the Well-Architected Framework Supports the Shared Responsibility Model

The Well-Architected Framework was built by AWS to provide a framework for cloud architects to build a secure, high-performing, resilient, and efficient infrastructure.[10] This framework can be used for a variety of applications and workloads. The six pillars that the Well-Architected Framework is built on are Operational Excellence, Reliability, Performance Efficiency, Cost Optimization, Sustainability, and the focus of this book – Security.

---

[10] https://aws.amazon.com/architecture/well-architected/?wa-lens-whitepapers.sort-by=item.additionalFields.sortDate&wa-lens-whitepapers.sort-order=desc&wa-guidance-whitepapers.sort-by=item.additionalFields.sortDate&wa-guidance-whitepapers.sort-order=desc

Remember the topic of trade-offs we reviewed earlier? The Well-Architected Framework helps you understand the trade-offs for decisions you make when building your AWS infrastructure. The Security Pillar[11] focuses on how to take advantage of cloud technologies to take advantage of resources to protect data, systems, and assets to improve the overall security of your workload.

Security Foundations

AWS provides resources and services to help customers build a more secure architecture. Some fundamental design principles include the following:

- Implement a strong identity foundation using IAM.

- Enable traceability by using CloudTrail.

- Apply security at all layers using a defense-in-depth approach using services like a Web Application Firewall (WAF), Network ACLs (NACLs), Security Groups, Service Control Policies (SCPs), and KMS.

- Automate security best practices such as the principle of least privilege.

- Protect your data in transit and at rest by using encryption and access controls.

---

[11] https://docs.aws.amazon.com/wellarchitected/latest/security-pillar/welcome.html

Identity and Access Management

Access management to services should be provided on a "need-to-know" and "need-to-do" basis. IAM policies can be applied at a granular level to specify actions, resources, and users. As you read earlier about AWS performing regular reviews of their personnel to ensure access was still needed for a job function, organizations should adopt similar habits. Job roles updating, people leaving, and organization restructuring are examples of how IAM policies that are not reviewed regularly can allow more access than necessary. Identity management can be broken into two different types of identities:

1) Human identities represent individuals and their roles within an organization.

2) Machine identities can include your workload applications, operational tools, and components that require an identity to make a request to AWS services.

Permissions management can manage different permission levels for both human and machine identities. Different policy types can be used to grant access to different types of resources:

- Identity-based policies are used with IAM identities (users, groups, or roles).

- Resource-based policies are attached to a resource.

- Permissions boundaries use a managed policy to establish a maximum number of permissions an administrator can set.

- Attribute-based access control allows you to grant permissions based on tags on an IAM principle.

- Organization Service Control Policies (SCPs) are used in AWS Organizations or organizational units (OUs) to define the maximum permissions for account members.

- Session policies allow limited permissions per session based on a role or identity-based policies.

Detection

Detection enables you to identify a potential security threat, misconfiguration, or unexpected behavior. It consists of two parts:

- Detection of an unexpected or unwanted configuration change can take in different stages of the application lifecycle.

- Detection of unexpected behavior can be monitored and notifications sent based on API calls made.

Infrastructure Protection

Infrastructure protection is a key part of security. We've already explored the different layers of protection that AWS provides for its facilities. This also includes all Availability Zones (AZs) in a Region using high-bandwidth, low-latency networking that provides high throughput between AZs. Customers can take advantage of this network and infrastructure protection to reach high levels of availability by building their cloud architecture using Multi-AZ or Multi-Region services. Infrastructure protection can be broken into two areas:

- **Protecting networks** requires planning and managing network design to provide isolation and boundaries for resources in your workload.

- **Protecting compute** is done based on the type of compute resource used. Despite different protections for different computing resources, they have common elements such as strategies for defense in depth, vulnerability management, reduction in attack surface, and automation.

Data Protection

Data protection uses foundational practices to influence security protocols. Data protection can be done using different approaches:

- **Data classification** provides a way to categorize organizational data based on sensitivity to help determine the appropriate protection.

- **Protecting data at rest** can be done by using both tokenization and encryption techniques.

- **Protecting data in transit** by using practices like using an SSL certificate, protocols, and security groups, to name just a few.

Incident Response

Incident response is imperative because nothing is foolproof. Despite best efforts and best practices, the chance of an incident occuring does remain, and an organization should have a response plan in place. Figure 2-8 shows the Security Development Lifecycle. The first step is Prevention, but it's not always effective and must go through the cycle of Detection → Response → Analysis and taking the lessons learned to develop new preventative measures.

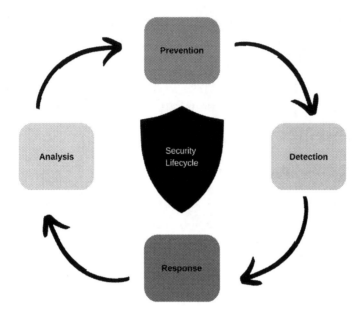

Figure 2-8. *Security Development Lifecycle*

While the best defense is a good offense, sometimes your defense needs to be ready and able to perform. The Well-Architected Framework is one tool that you can use to ensure the offense team and the defense team are educated and ready to perform.

Describe the Purpose and Responsibilities for Identity and Access Management

Identity and Access Management is one of the free resources with AWS. It can be used to establish the very basic foundational practices of maintaining architecture security – the principle of least privilege. When teaching this subject, I use the analogy of don't leave the chicken coop door open so the fox can come in. AWS has established strict policy rules in terms of explicit allows and implicit denies, but it's still ultimately the customer's responsibility to use this resource correctly.

AWS provides a list of best practices when using IAM to specify who can do what to which resource and under what conditions. These best practices include the following:

- **Use temporary credentials** by requiring users to use temporary credentials with an identity provider to gain access to AWS. These temporary credentials are assigned by using IAM roles.

- **Require MFA** for IAM users or root user access to an account.

- **Rotate access keys regularly**: While temporary credentials are recommended (and, as you may remember, practiced by AWS for access in their data centers), if a long-term credential is needed by granting an access key, rotate the access keys regularly.

- **Safeguard your root user credentials**: Remember that a root user has the master key for all levels of access to all resources in AWS. The root user should only be used for limited as-needed applications, and assigning an IAM Admin role can take the place of many high-level tasks without exposing root credentials.

- **Principle of least privilege**: If access is not needed to do their job, access is not needed – period. Granting the least privilege is a fundamental best practice in maintaining a secure environment. AWS provides a list of managed policies that can be applied to an IAM user, group, or role that covers a variety of scenarios for individual resources. This can be a great resource to implement easily without custom writing rules. When access needs to be more customized, Customer Managed Policies can be created, or inline policies can be used as well.

59

Summary

In this chapter, we reviewed more about who exactly is responsible again for security. The default reference is AWS's Shared Responsibility Model, but it can be a little ambiguous because depending on the resources you are using, there is an "it depends" factor. Microsoft Azure adopts a different approach in displaying the shared responsibilities for IaaS, PaaS, and SaaS, which can be helpful when first learning to understand how different services have different responsibilities.

With the changing technologies also comes the need to change security strategies. The CIA has been a long-established foundation for maintaining a secure network, and a new DIE model can address changing technologies and capabilities.

The responsibility is ultimately shared between AWS and the customer. AWS goes to great lengths to ensure that they are managing the security of its infrastructure across the world. AWS has also designed the Well-Architected Framework. This provides customers a framework they can refer to so that customers can build a stronger and more secure architecture.

CHAPTER 3

How Do I Build a Secure Architecture?

AWS provides a wide array of resources and services to help its customers maintain a secure environment. In this chapter, we will review how customers can use these resources for their AWS account and also for specific services like computing, storage, networking, and databases. We will also cover how data is encrypted at rest and in transit and how unauthorized configuration changes can trigger an alarm.

Cybersecurity

It's no surprise that cybersecurity is one of the most prevalent concerns in our nation (and around the world) today. In May 2021, the President of the United States signed an Executive Order on Improving the Nation's Cybersecurity that states *"The United States faces persistent and increasingly sophisticated malicious cyber campaigns that threaten the public sector, the private sector, and ultimately the American people's security and privacy. The Federal Government must improve its efforts to identify, deter, protect against, detect, and respond to these actions and actors."*[1]

---

[1] https://nvlpubs.nist.gov/nistpubs/SpecialPublications/NIST.SP.800-160v1r1.pdf

© Tasha Penwell 2023
T. Penwell, *Beginning AWS Security*, https://doi.org/10.1007/978-1-4842-9681-3_3

In order to support the Executive Order, the National Institute of Standards and Technology (NIST) states that the following needs to be met:

- Identify stakeholder assets and protection needs.

- Provide protection that aligns with the impact of asset loss and is correlated with threat and adversary capabilities.

- Develop scenarios and model the complexity of systems to provide a basis to build, manage, and address any uncertainty regarding security measures.

- Adopt an engineering-based approach that addresses concerns of trustworthiness.

With the rise of cloud computing services and the increasing adoption of cloud computing, having a framework can help identify what decisions and trade-offs need to be made. The Well-Architected Framework[2] is made up of six pillars – Performance Efficiency, Reliability, Operational Excellence, Cost Optimization, Security, and Sustainability. The mnemonic I like to use is "Building a Well-Architected Framework is a PROCeSS":

> P – Performance Efficiency
>
> R – Reliability
>
> O – Operational Excellence
>
> C – Cost Optimization
>
> S – Security
>
> S – Sustainability

---

[2] https://aws.amazon.com/architecture/well-architected

In this book, we will be focusing on the Security Pillar and identifying what resources and methods can be used to secure the different services.

AWS Security Services

Recall from Chapter 2, there are three different cloud models. They are IaaS, PaaS, and SaaS. With an understanding of the three service models, it's time to identify what AWS services can be used for different resources in those models. Some security services are universally applied as a best practice regardless of the type of resource used. Let's explore those first as they help set the basic fundamentals of a secure environment.

General Security Services That Are Automatically Available at No Charge

AWS Identity and Access Management (IAM)

- IAM is a web service for securely controlling access to AWS resources. This is for internal users or other resources, such as an EC2 instance, not the end users of an application. IAM is used to control what users, roles, or groups can access a resource and what actions they can take on that resource.

- Helps enforce the principle of least privilege (PoLP) by limiting user access based on what is needed to perform their job function.

AWS Shield

- Provides protection against DDoS attacks on the network

AWS CloudTrail

- A monitoring service, not a security service

- Monitors API calls made in an account

Services That Provide Protection in VPCs

Security Groups

- Security feature for VPCs

- Act as a virtual firewall to allow or deny inbound or outbound traffic at the resource (i.e., EC2 instance) level

Network Access Control Lists

- Security feature for VPCs

- Allow or deny both inbound and outbound traffic at the subnet level

VPC Flow Logs

- Captures information about the IP traffic going to and from the network interfaces in a VPC

Security Services That Are Not Enabled by Default and Can Accrue Charges

Amazon Detective

- Helps cloud administrators perform a root cause analysis by analyzing, investigating, and quickly identifying the root cause of security findings or suspicious activities

- Uses machine learning, statistical analysis, and graph theory to generate visualizations to help conduct security investigations more efficiently

AWS Firewall Manager

- Simplifies administration and maintenance across multiple accounts and resources for a variety of protections (AWS Web Application Firewall, AWS Shield Advanced, Amazon VPC Security Groups, AWS Network Firewall, and Amazon Route 53 Resolver DNS Firewall)

- Allows you to set up the services once and apply them automatically across AWS accounts and resources

- Provides centralized monitoring of DDoS attacks across your organization

Amazon GuardDuty

- Continuous security monitoring service

- Helps identify unexpected and malicious activity

- Analyzes and processes data sources like AWS
  CloudTrail data events for Amazon S3 logs, CloudTrail
  management event logs, DNS logs, Amazon EBS
  volume data, Kubernetes audit logs, Amazon VPC flow
  logs, and RDS login activity

- Uses threat intelligence feeds such as a list of malicious
  IP addresses and domains to identify malicious activity

- Monitors AWS account access behavior to identify any
  anomalies that could be a sign of account compromise

- Informs you of the status of the AWS environment by
  producing security findings that you can view in the
  GuardDuty console or Amazon CloudWatch Events or
  export to S3 buckets

- Can integrate with AWS Security Hub and Amazon
  Detective

AWS IAM Identity Center

- Provides one place to create or connect workforce
  (human) users and manage their access to all their
  AWS accounts and applications that support SAML 2.0

- Provides a centralized place to create and connect
  workforce users and centrally manage their access on
  Identity Center–enabled applications

- Allows for multi-account permissions you can plan
  for and centrally implements IAM permissions across
  multiple AWS accounts at one time

- Creates granular permissions based on common job
  roles or custom permissions to meet security needs

Amazon Inspector

- Security vulnerability assessment service

- Helps improve the security and compliance of AWS resources

- Assesses resources for vulnerabilities or deviations from best practices

- Produces a list of findings prioritized by level of severity

- Automatically discovers EC2 instances, container images in ECR, and AWS Lambda functions for known vulnerabilities and unintended network exposure

AWS Secrets Manager

- Allows users to replace hardcoded credentials in code (such as passwords) with an API call to Secrets Manager

- Can be configured to automatically rotate the secret for you according to a specified schedule

- Allows secrets such as credentials to be updated more regularly without needing to update applications individually

AWS Security Hub

- Provides you with a comprehensive view of the state of security of your AWS resources

- Collects security data from across AWS accounts, services, and supported third-party partner products

- Helps you analyze your security trends and identify the highest priority security issues

AWS Config

- A monitoring service, not a security service

- Provides a detailed view of resources and configurations of resources in an AWS account

Network Protection

AWS Network Firewall

- Stateful, managed, network firewall

- IDS (intrusion detection system) and IPS (intrusion prevention system) for VPC

- Filters traffic going to and coming from an Internet Gateway (IGW), Network Address Translation (NAT) gateway, or over a virtual private network (VPN) or AWS Direct Connect (DX)

Data Protection

Amazon Macie

- Fully managed data security and data privacy service

- Uses machine learning and pattern matching to help discover, monitor, and protect sensitive data in S3

Mobile and Web Applications

Amazon Cognito

- Allows you to add user sign-up, sign-in, and access control to web and mobile applications

- Supports SAML 2 and OpenID Connect to allow SSO via social identity providers

- Utilizes user pools and identity pools

  - User pools are user directories that provide sign-up and sign-in options for application end users.

  - Identity pools are used to grant users access to other AWS services.

AWS Web Application Firewall

- Allows you to monitor web requests that are forwarded to Amazon CloudFront distributions or an Application Load Balancer

- Can be used to block or allow requests based on conditions you specify

As you can see, there are a variety of services available for organizations of all size to use to create a secure cloud environment. Earlier in this book, you read about three companies that had exposed vulnerabilities – Pegasus Airlines, Accenture, and Capital One. You may remember that the common element among them all was a vulnerability in an S3 bucket. With the variety of services that are available to monitor, detect, notify, and even fix a vulnerability, why do these vulnerabilities continue to exist?

There are two things that contribute to this inefficient use of security and monitoring tools – lack of resources and lack of training.

Resources

Resources can include money, time, or both. Money and time are finite resources for all organizations, and not all the security resources provided by AWS are free of charge. Table 3-1 provides information on which resources are free, have a "freemium" version, and what will generate a bill to your account.

Table 3-1. *List of service with free tier options*

Service	Free Tier	Freemium	Paid Service
IAM	Yes	No	No
Amazon Detective	Free 30-day trial	No	Price based on the volume of data ingested from logs. Charged per GB ingested per account/region/month
AWS Firewall Manager	No	No	Monthly fee starting at $100 per Region
Amazon GuardDuty	Free 30-day trial	No	Price based on the volume of both analyzed service logs and data scanned for malware
AWS IAM Identity Center	Yes	No	No
Amazon Inspector	Free 30-day trial	No	Monthly costs are determined based on the different workloads (EC2, ECR, Lambda) scanned
Amazon Secrets Manager	Free 30-day trial	No	$0.40 per secret per month
AWS Security Hub	Free 30-day trial	No	Price based on the number of security checks and the quantity of ingested findings each month

(continued)

Table 3-1. (*continued*)

Service	Free Tier	Freemium	Paid Service
AWS Shield	Yes (AWS Shield)	Yes (AWS Shield)	AWS Shield Advanced requires a 1-year commitment at a monthly fee of $3000.00 per AWS Organization. Additional charges for data transfer can apply
AWS Config	No	Yes	Price based on the number of configuration items recorded, active Config rule evaluations, and the number of conformance pack evaluations
AWS CloudTrail	Yes	Yes	CloudTrail Lake provides additional ingestion and storage
Security Groups	Yes	No	No
Network Access Control Lists	Yes	No	No
VPC Flow Logs	Yes	No	No
Amazon Macie	Free 30-day trial	No	Pricing is based on S3 objects monitored and quantity of data inspected

(*continued*)

Table 3-1. (*continued*)

Service	Free Tier	Freemium	Paid Service
Amazon Cognito	Yes	No	Pricing based on what is used beyond the monthly active user limits in the free tier
AWS Web Application Firewall	Yes	No	Pricing is based on the number of web access control lists, the number of rules per web ACL, and the number of web requests received

As you can see from Table 3-1, while there is a great deal of security and monitoring services available, they do have an impact on the monthly operating expenses in your AWS account.

When teaching about cloud security services covering AWS security best practices and reviewing case studies like Pegasus, Accenture, and Capital One, we discuss why organizations of this size let their data become vulnerable. One thing I find interesting about security in the cloud is that it's an area you invest in to see nothing happen - no attacks, no vulnerabilities, no alarms. Oftentimes, organizations and individuals fail to justify the expense or inconvenience of securing an environment or providing cloud security training until there is an attack. Despite reports and case studies that make the news, it can be difficult to approve an expense based on "what-ifs." A risk assessment can help identify the likelihood of an event happening and its impact on the business.

Another reason that businesses could overlook utilizing AWS security or monitoring resources is a lack of knowledge. AWS customers can be young entrepreneurs wearing multiple hats who decide to utilize managed services to allow them to focus on their business and are unaware of their remaining responsibilities according to the Shared Responsibility Model.

They can be large organizations with administrators who are not properly trained on or updated on cloud services they can use to secure their environment.

Cloud Adoption Framework

When identifying responsibilities of ownership in larger organizations as they decide to adopt or migrate to the cloud, the Cloud Adoption Framework (CAF) can provide guidance and perspectives that should be used to help appropriately delegate and assign ownership. The Cloud Adoption Framework is made up of 6 perspectives and 47 capabilities (Figure 3-1).

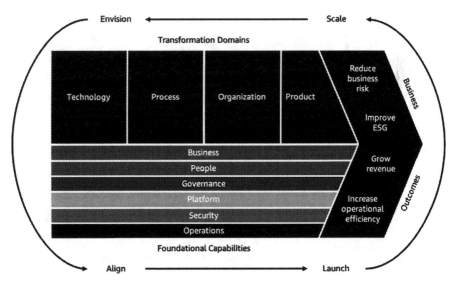

Figure 3-1. *AWS's Cloud Adoption Framework 3.0*

The six perspectives in the CAF are Business, People, Governance, Platform, Security, and Operations. These six foundations help support the value chain that starts with Technology. Technology transformations enable Process transformation which enables Organizational transformation which leads to Product transformation. This value chain can lead to business outcomes of reduced business risk, improved performance, increased revenue, and operational efficiency.

Security Perspective

The security perspective helps an organization achieve in maintaining the CIA triad of data and workloads. It is made up of nine capabilities that the responsibility for obtaining and maintaining can fall to the CISO, CCO, internal audit leaders, security architects, and security engineers.

The nine capabilities of the security perspective are as follows: security governance, security assurance, identity and access management, threat detection, vulnerability management, infrastructure protection, data protection, application security, and incident response.

Security Perspective Capability #1 – Security Governance

- Develops, maintains, and communicates security roles, responsibilities, accountabilities, policies, processes, and procedures.

- Ensures there are clear lines of accountability for the effectiveness of the security program.

- Understanding assets, security risks, and compliance requirements can help prioritize security efforts.

- Understand the organization's responsibility for security in the cloud.

- Risk assessments or a risk matrix can help identify the likelihood of a risk and its impact so that appropriate choices can be made.

Security Perspective Capability #2 – Security Assurance

- Continuously monitor, evaluate, manage, and improve the effectiveness of security and privacy programs.

- Organizations and stakeholders need assurance that controls have been properly implemented to meet requirements in line with business objectives and risk tolerance.

Security Perspective Capability #3 – Identity and Access Management

- Manage identities and permissions at scale.

- Validate that the correct people and resources/ machines have access to the right resources under the right conditions.

Security Perspective Capability #4 – Threat Detection

- Understand and identify potential security misconfigurations, threats, or unexpected behaviors to help prioritize protective controls.

- Organizational security professionals need to agree on tactical, operational, and strategic intelligence goals and methods that include mining data sources, processing and analyzing data, and disseminating and operationalizing insights.

Security Perspective Capability #5 – Vulnerability Management

- Identify, classify, remediate, and mitigate security vulnerabilities on a continuous basis.

- Prioritize remediation action based on vulnerability risk.

Security Perspective Capability #6 – Data Protection

- Maintain visibility and control over data and how it is accessed.

- Use data classification to help identify criticality and sensitivity of data.

- Encrypt data at rest and in transit.

- Establish lifecycle policies.

- Use AWS Organizations and store sensitive data in separate accounts.

- Utilize machine learning to discover, classify, and protect sensitive data.

Security Perspective Capability #7 – Infrastructure Protection

- Validate that the systems and services are protected against unintended and unauthorized access from potential vulnerabilities.

- Leverage defense-in-depth methods at individual layers.

Security Perspective Capability #8 – Application Security

- Detect and address security vulnerabilities during the SDLC.

- Use a secure software engineering process[3] that incorporates threat modeling into the different phases of the SDLC.

- Use automation and minimize the need for human intervention for security-related tasks.

Security Perspective Capability #9 – Incident Response

- Reduce potential harm by responding to security incidents.

- Educate the security operations and incident response teams on resources and best practices and how the organization will be using them.

- Simulate an event with "game days" and analyze responses and outcomes.

---

[3] https://versprite.com/blog/security-operations/software-development-lifecycle-threat-modeling/#:~:text=Threat%20modeling%20within%20the%20SDLC,design%20countermeasures%20to%20protect%20them

The nine capabilities and their descriptions are shown in Table 3-2.[4]

Table 3-2. *Cloud Adoption Framework capabilities*

Security Capability	Description
Security Governance	Develop and communicate security roles, responsibilities, policies, processes, and procedures
Threat Detection	Understand and identify potential security misconfigurations, threats, or unexpected behaviors
Data Protection	Maintain visibility and control over data and how it is accessed and used in an organization
Security Assurance	Monitor, evaluate, manage, and improve the effectiveness of security and privacy programs
Vulnerability Management	Continuously identify, classify, remediate, and mitigate security vulnerabilities
Application Security	Detect and address security vulnerabilities during the software development process
Identity and Access Management	Manage identities and permissions at scale
Infrastructure Protection	Validate that systems and services within your workload are protected
Incident Response	Reduce potential harm by effectively responding to security incidents

When teaching about the Cloud Adoption Framework (focuses on people and roles) and the Well-Architected Framework (focuses on best practices), I like to have my students identify the connection between the

---

[4] https://docs.aws.amazon.com/whitepapers/latest/overview-aws-cloud-adoption-framework/security-perspective.html

two to better understand how the responsibilities of the individuals can take advantage of the resources available to build a secure architecture. Table 3-3 provides some possibilities.

Table 3-3. *Cloud Adoption Framework capabilities and AWS resources to help support*

Security Capability	Description	AWS Resources
Security Governance	Develop and communicate security roles, responsibilities, policies, processes, and procedures	• IAM is used to manage permissions to users to help align to PoLP • AWS IAM Identity Center manages IAM permissions for multiple accounts in an Organization • Amazon Secrets Manager manages secrets to protect access to applications, services, and IT resources to align with security policies and procedures • AWS CloudTrail is used to capture all API calls made so they can be audited to ensure that role permissions are correct and align with policies

(*continued*)

Table 3-3. (*continued*)

Security Capability	Description	AWS Resources
Threat Detection	Understand and identify potential security misconfigurations, threats, or unexpected behaviors	• Amazon GuardDuty continuously monitors AWS accounts and workloads for malicious activity and delivers reports on findings • Amazon Inspector scans workloads for vulnerabilities from misconfigurations • AWS Security Hub performs security best practice checks, aggregates alerts to find misconfigurations or threats • AWS Shield is a managed DDoS protection service that can mitigate DDoS threats • Amazon Config provides a detailed view of AWS resource configuration, configuration history and configuration change notifications that do not align with Config rules

(*continued*)

Table 3-3. (*continued*)

Security Capability	Description	AWS Resources
Data Protection	Maintain visibility and control over data and how it is accessed and used in an organization	• AWS CloudTrail is used to capture all API calls made. They can be audited to ensure that role permissions are being used as expected • Amazon Macie is a data security service that discovers sensitive data using machine learning and pattern matching • IAM is used to manage permissions to users to help align to PoLP to limit data access • AWS IAM Identity Center manages IAM permissions for multiple accounts in an Organization to limit data access

(*continued*)

Table 3-3. (*continued*)

Security Capability	Description	AWS Resources
Security Assurance	Monitor, evaluate, manage, and improve the effectiveness of security and privacy programs	• AWS Firewall Manager is a management service that allows you to configure and manage firewall rules to ensure security is managed • Amazon GuardDuty continuously monitors AWS accounts and workloads for malicious activity and delivers reports on findings • Amazon Inspector scans workloads for vulnerabilities • AWS Security Hub performs security best practice checks, aggregates alerts, and enables automated remediation • AWS Web Application Firewall monitors HTTP/S requests to a protected web application resource

(*continued*)

Table 3-3. (*continued*)

Security Capability	Description	AWS Resources
Vulnerability Management	Continuously identify, classify, remediate, and mitigate security vulnerabilities	• Amazon GuardDuty continuously monitors AWS accounts and workloads for malicious activity and delivers reports on findings • Amazon Inspector scans workloads for software vulnerabilities • Amazon Config provides AWS resource and configuration history and configuration change notifications to remediate security vulnerabilities
Application Security	Detect and address security vulnerabilities during the software development process	• Amazon Detective collects log data and uses ML and analysis to perform security investigations • Amazon Inspector scans workloads for software vulnerabilities

(*continued*)

Table 3-3. (*continued*)

Security Capability	Description	AWS Resources
Identity and Access Management	Manage identities and permissions at scale	• IAM is used to manage permissions to users to help align to PoLP • AWS IAM Identity Center manages IAM permissions for multiple accounts in an Organization • Amazon Secrets Manager manages secrets to protect access to applications, services, and IT resources to align with security policies and procedures • Amazon Cognito can control identities and permissions by using user pools and identity pools

(*continued*)

Table 3-3. (*continued*)

Security Capability	Description	AWS Resources
Infrastructure Protection	Validate that systems and services within your workload are protected	• AWS Firewall Manager is a management service that allows you to configure and manage firewall rules to ensure security • Amazon GuardDuty continuously monitors AWS accounts and workloads for malicious activity and delivers reports on findings • Amazon Inspector scans workloads for software vulnerabilities • AWS Security Hub performs security best practice checks, aggregates alerts, and enables automated remediation • Amazon Config provides AWS resource and configuration history and configuration change notifications to remediate security vulnerabilities • Security Groups are placed at the resource level to control network traffic in and out • Network Access Control Lists are at the subnet level and can be used to control network traffic in and out • VPC Flow Logs are used for network monitoring, forensics security analysis, and expense optimization

(*continued*)

Table 3-3. (*continued*)

Security Capability	Description	AWS Resources
Incident Response	Reduce potential harm by effectively responding to security incidents	• Amazon Detective collects log data from sources to conduct efficient security investigations • AWS Security Hub performs best practice checks, aggregates alerts, and enables automated remediation • AWS Config provides resource inventory with configuration history and change notifications to respond to potentially harmful security incidents and automate changes based on config rules

Let's put some of what you covered in this chapter into practice by analyzing the Capital One Data Breach introduced earlier in this book. As a recap, an outside individual gained unauthorized access and obtained certain types of personal information about Capital One customers or those who applied for credit card products.

Recall that one of the security perspective capabilities focused on infrastructure protection and applying a defense-in-depth approach. Defense in depth (DiD) is a security approach to apply security mechanisms and controls throughout the layers of a computer network to protect the confidentiality, integrity, and availability of the network and its data.

The following are the details discovered by the FBI that are available from the Criminal Complaint from July 29, 2019:[5]

- There was a network intrusion into servers rented or contracted by Capital One (this was later to be revealed servers belonged to AWS).

- Records obtained from Capital One indicate that the IP addresses used by the intruder were controlled by a company that provides VPN services.

- Capital One determined that the attacker was able to access the IP address for a specific server.

- Firewall misconfigurations permitted commands to reach and be executed by the server which enabled access to S3 buckets storing data.

- The attacker was able to obtain security credentials for an account that enabled access to certain Capital One folders.

- The attacker was able to list the names of folders or buckets of data in Capital One's storage space.

- The attacker was able to extract data from the buckets.

- The attackers used TOR exit nodes and a number of connections from IP addresses beginning with 46.246.

- Capital One confirmed that some of the data copied from their data folders were encrypted, and other information was stored as plaintext.

---

[5] www.documentcloud.org/documents/6224689-Capital-One-breach-criminal-complaint.html

In summary, Capital One was storing confidential data in S3 buckets. Not all the data stored was encrypted. An attacker was able to get past the firewall unnoticed by Capital One and extract data from the S3 bucket.

Recall what the Security Pillar's seven design principles for security in the cloud are:

1. Implement a strong identity foundation.

2. Enable traceability.

3. Apply security at all layers.

4. Automate security best practices.

5. Protect data in transit and at rest.

6. Keep people away from data.

7. Prepare for security events.

If Capital One had referred to the Security Pillar in the Well-Architected Framework, what changes do you think they would have made? They may look something like what you see in Table 3-4.

Table 3-4. *Security Pillar design principles and AWS resources to support*

Design Principle	Known Vulnerability	AWS Resource to Use
Implement a strong identity foundation	The attacker was able to access the S3 buckets without proper authentication	• IAM to specify which users can access resources • Secrets Manager to rotate secrets more frequently using automation
Enable traceability	The attacker was able to infiltrate and extract data without triggering any alarms	• AWS GuardDuty can analyze unexpected and malicious activity. It monitors account access to identify any anomalies • AWS CloudTrail to identify abnormal API calls
Apply security at all layers	The attacker was able to penetrate the firewalls and then see the data stored in plaintext	• AWS Network Firewall that provides control over network traffic • Amazon Macie can discover, monitor, and protect sensitive data • S3 bucket policies to limit access

(*continued*)

Table 3-4. (*continued*)

Design Principle	Known Vulnerability	AWS Resource to Use
Automate security best practices	The attacker was able to access data after unauthorized entry to an S3 bucket	• Config can detect any changes to configuration and automatically correct them based on rules. Can also send a notification to notify you of the configuration change
Protect data in transit and at rest	Data was left unencrypted in the bucket	• Announced in January 2023, AWS will encrypt all new objects by default using SSE-S3
Keep people away from data	The attacker was able to access the data	• Resources like IAM can limit access and can be used to explicitly deny users based on parameters • Network firewalls can also limit access to unauthorized users based on policies
Prepare for security events	Capital One responded to the attack once it learned of it If victims were protected by GDPR or PIPL based out of Europe or China, respectively, Capital One would need to prepare for these regulations on data privacy protections	(Intentionally left blank)

AWS Systems Manager

AWS Systems Manager (SSM) is an operation hub for AWS applications and resources. In Figure 3-2, you can see the capabilities of SSM include the following:

- Group your resources and save them into groups

- Gain operational insights from the dashboard interface

- Mitigate issues by performing operations directly on the resource groups

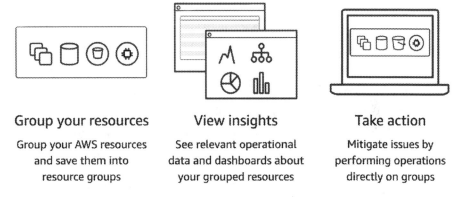

Group your resources

Group your AWS resources and save them into resource groups

View insights

See relevant operational data and dashboards about your grouped resources

Take action

Mitigate issues by performing operations directly on groups

Figure 3-2. *AWS Systems Manager*

The single dashboard interface allows for a secure end-to-end management solution that can support hybrid and multicloud environments.

With Systems Manager, customers are able to automate common and repetitive IT operations and tasks. With SSM Automation, playbooks are used to manage resources at scale.[6]

---

[6] https://aws.amazon.com/systems-manager/features/#:~:text=AWS%20
Systems%20Manager%20allows%20you,multiple%20accounts%20and%20AWS%20
Regions

AWS Systems Manager Automation

Using SSM Automation, customers are able to take advantage of using runbooks to perform tasks with less manual efforts. This can include solutions to help deploy, configure, and manage resources at scale which can automate common tasks and enhance operational security by reducing human error.

AWS Security Lake

AWS Security Lake became generally available in May 2023 and provides centralized access to security data from AWS environments, SaaS providers, and on-premise solutions, in addition to hybrid and multicloud environments. This data is stored in a specialized data lake stored in the customer's S3 account.

Security Lake normalizes and combines data from AWS and other security data resources to help increase visibility and respond to security events more timely. Advantages of using Security Lake are as follows:

- Facilitation of security investigations with improved visibility. This is achieved by aggregating, normalizing, and optimizing the data stored in a single security data lake.

- Simplifies compliance monitoring and reporting by centralizing security data into one or more rollup Regions which can help meet compliance requirements.

- Analyzes multiple years of security data quickly and helps security teams gain insights to take appropriate measures quickly.

- Unified security data management across hybrid
  and multicloud environments. Aids with providing a
  better understanding and response to threats by using
  security-related logs and various data sources.

Security Lake helps organizations provide a centralized view to analyze security data. With this single-view application, they can spend more time protecting the environment and workloads and less time looking through multiple data resources.

Summary

In this chapter, you learned about the frameworks that AWS provides to help identify roles and resources that need to be included to build a secure infrastructure. Security never sleeps, and as cloud professionals, it is imperative that awareness and understanding of delegated responsibilities for resources used are reviewed with everyone on the team.

CHAPTER 4

Security Is Not Built in a Day

Your network and cloud environment is completely secure and self-automated when cyberattacks stop advancing and all human errors stop. In other words, security never stops, and it is never completely built. Security starts with the basic fundamentals of authentication and authorization and builds from there to preventative and discovery tactics to thwart attacks.

Your environment's ability to be proactive and reactive to vulnerabilities and attacks plays a role in its security posture.

What Is Security Posture?

Security posture can be compared to your own physical posture. You know that good posture can portray confidence and prevents damage to your body. Maintaining a good security posture also has benefits for the organization. Security posture addresses the following questions:[1]

- How visible and aware are you of your assets?

- What proactive measures are in place to reduce the attack surface?

---

[1] www.balbix.com/insights/what-is-cyber-security-posture/

T. Penwell, *Beginning AWS Security*, https://doi.org/10.1007/978-1-4842-9681-3_4

- What controls and processes are in place to monitor and protect an organization from an attack?

- What strategies are in place to react and recover from an attack?

- How is automation built into the security program?

Standing tall with good physical posture can portray confidence to the world, and answering the preceding questions can also build confidence in your organization's ability to prevent and, if necessary, appropriately recover from a cyberattack. Developing an effective security posture requires an organization to be both proactive and reactive to protect its assets and reduce its liabilities.

AWS Security Hub

AWS Security Hub is AWS's cloud security posture management (CSPM) service that has several benefits to the customer. These benefits include the following:

- Performs security best practice checks

- Aggregates alerts into one dashboard

- Enables automated remediation

- Reduces alarm fatigue and improves response to cyber threats

With the Security Hub, customers can reduce time and resources spent in collecting and understanding the findings generated. This can help security professionals prioritize the most important findings and reduce alarm fatigue. Alarm fatigue can lead to overwhelmed cybersecurity personnel who are conflicted with managing alarms and can become desensitized to them.

Another benefit of using Security Hub is that it can run continuous configuration and security checks at an account level using industry standards and AWS best practices. From that, a readiness score is provided and can identify specific accounts and resources that require more attention from the security personnel.

How Visible and Aware Are You of Your Assets?

Whether your applications are supported by on-premise, hybrid, or public cloud options, it is important to know what assets your organization currently has so that it can ensure it is protected. An unknown asset is an unmonitored and unprotected asset – which means it is now a vulnerability waiting to be exploited. Defining your attack surface is an important step to protection. The attack surface is a combination of asset inventory and attack vectors. To organize and collect data on your assets, the following items need to be cataloged:

Assets

- Third-party assets

- Custom applications

- Managed services

- Unmanaged services

- Cloud-native applications

- Infrastructure

Location

- Geographical locations of physical equipment

- List of geographical areas in AWS's global infrastructure (Regions, AZ, Local Zone, Edge Locations, Direct Connect, etc.)

Business Criticality

- Identify what assets are critical for business operations

- Identify vulnerability risks for attack and availability

- Quantify business risk impact (i.e., time lost, revenue lost, etc.)

Current Security Measures

- Access management

- Firewalls

- Monitoring services

- Intrusion detection systems (IDS)

- Intrusion prevention systems (IPS)

Attack Vectors and Vulnerabilities

- Methods that attackers can use to infiltrate

- Vulnerabilities identified from simulated attacks

- Personnel training

Automation

- Current automation practices

- Identify where automation can be added

Proactive and Reactive in Cloud Security

When I teach about security, I explain to my students that cybersecurity and cloud security are areas where you spend a lot of resources and time monitoring and auditing hoping to see nothing happen. Too often, organizations decide to cut corners on their security measures and focus on their business operations. While it is important to focus on business operations, to continue to have a business also requires ensuring that the data, network, process, and operations are protected from infiltration, exfiltration, and overall compromise.

Note   In addition to AWS Security Hub, AWS Marketplace provides a variety of AWS approved marketplace vendors that can provide additional tools to aid with cloud security posture management and are ready to integrate with AWS. Learn more about approved AWS CSPM third-party providers at `https://aws.amazon.com/ marketplace/solutions/security/cloud-security- posture-management`.

AWS's default reference model is the Shared Responsibility Model. You already know that the Shared Responsibility Model provides some guidance on responsibility. This level of responsibility can also be based on the type of service used.

The following are some examples of how Snap, Volkswagen, and Twilio are taking proactive and reactive approaches to their security.

Snap

- Snap, Inc. (Snap) is a social media and camera company. It is best known for its augmented reality capabilities to create filters. The company's products include Camera, Communication, Spotlight, Stories, Snap Map, Memories, and Spectacles.

  Snap, Inc. is also an example of an organization that is being proactive about cloud security by using Amazon GuardDuty. In a short interview with Roger Zou (software engineer at Snap), he explained how GuardDuty's ability to perform intelligent threat detection services provides a degree of confidence in their overall network security. This allows for better use of resources to focus on business operations and scaling instead of spending more time searching for anomalies.[2]

How Can GuardDuty Help Protect Your Accounts?

GuardDuty[3] is a security monitoring service that analyzes and processes data sources that include logs from CloudTrail which tracks all API calls made in an AWS account. GuardDuty is activated quickly and simply and allows Snap and other customers to immediately begin analyzing all AWS accounts. GuardDuty will automatically and continuously monitor AWS workloads and resources and use machine learning to identify any anomalies and potential threats. These resources can include Amazon S3, database services, container workloads, instance workloads, accounts and users, and serverless services.

GuardDuty's findings are displayed in the console and can also be integrated with event management, workload systems, or automated remediation and prevention.

- **Improve security operations visibility** by discovering and analyzing compromised credentials or other suspicious activities.

- **Assist analysts in root cause analysis and remediation** by reviewing the metadata and affected resources and use Amazon Detective to determine the source of the vulnerability.

---

[2] https://pages.awscloud.com/aws-coffee-break-security-snap-how-to-protect-workloads.html

[3] https://docs.aws.amazon.com/guardduty/latest/ug/what-is-guardduty.html

- **Identify files containing malware** by scanning files used for virtual machines (EC2 instances) or container workloads running on EC2.

- **Detect and mitigate threats in your container environment** by identifying and profiling suspicious activity by reviewing Amazon EKS audit logs and runtime activity.

Volkswagen

- Volkswagen[4] is a German car manufacturer and also a customer of AWS that uses Amazon GuardDuty to protect its account. In addition to GuardDuty, it uses another service that provides a centralized view of all security findings. This tool is AWS Security Hub.

  Security Hub[5] provides a comprehensive look at all the security alerts and overall security posture of accounts. Security Hub works by running automatic security checks across all the accounts in an AWS environment. These checks consolidate and prioritize security findings from Amazon GuardDuty, Amazon Inspector, Amazon Macie, and other services. Customized actions can be programmed such as ticketing, chat, email, or using automation to remediate systems by integration with Amazon CloudWatch Events.

---

[4] https://aws.amazon.com/solutions/case-studies/volkswagen-group-guardduty/?did=cr_card&trk=cr_card

[5] https://aws.amazon.com/security-hub/

Twilio

- Twilio provides programmable communication tools worldwide and is considered a cloud Communications Platform as a Service (CPaaS). In July 2020, an article from Dark Reading[6] shared that attackers accessed an Amazon S3 bucket due to misconfiguration. In this attack, the attackers made unapproved changes to the TaskRouter JavaScript SDK. This SDK is used to help customers interact with TaskRouter which provides a routing engine to send tasks to agents or processes. This misconfigured file could have been cached by the user's browser or through a CDN on CloudFlare for up to 24 hours after the code was placed on the image.

  In the article, Twilio stated that when troubleshooting a problem it had in a system, they had changed the account settings and permissions for Amazon S3. Once the issue had been resolved, the account settings were not properly reset. Once this was found and corrected, Twilio reviewed their other AWS accounts and discovered other S3 accounts that were not properly configured for protection.

In two of the case studies shared, you learned how services like GuardDuty and Security Hub can offset the need for manual monitoring of accounts. GuardDuty uses machine learning to perform intelligent threat protection services, which allows its customers to focus on building

---

[6]www.darkreading.com/cloud/twilio-security-incident-shows-danger-of-misconfigured-s3-buckets

continued innovation in their products and services. Security Hub provides its customers the ability to see a holistic view of the account's security for easier findings of anomalies that may appear.

The Twilio case study, on the other hand, is an all-too-common story of accidental misconfigurations which could leave an organization vulnerable to a hidden attack.

Twilio's Incident Report[7] describes the incident that resulted in this vulnerability. The highlights of the incidents are the following:

- The TaskRouter JS SDK is a library that allows customers to interact with Twilio TaskRouter. This library is stored in Amazon Simple Storage Service (S3).

- Twilio TaskRouter provides an attribute-based routing engine to route tasks to agents or processes.

- On July 19, 2020, they became aware of a modification made to the JavaScript library that is used in the application.

- Approximately eight hours after the modification was done, an alert was received regarding the modified file.

- Due to the misconfiguration in the S3 bucket, an attacker was able to inject code that left users vulnerable to Magecart[8] attacks that focus on skimming customers' data.

- The attack was most likely due to being opportunistic – taking advantage of vulnerabilities in S3 configurations.

---

[7] www.twilio.com/blog/incident-report-taskrouter-js-sdk-july-2020
[8] https://netacea.com/glossary/magecart/#:~:text=Magecart%20is%20a%20form%20of,Checkout%20or%20Order%20Confirmation%20page

- Upon further investigation, Twilio identified additional
  S3 buckets that were also left vulnerable due to the
  same misconfiguration.

Twilio is a great example to highlight that changes, updates, and dependencies are a normal part of business operations. These can come from internal changes to the code base, updated features, or security updates. Regardless of the need, this is an example of why security is a never-ending, always-looking process. Twilio has learned from this process and has adopted a more proactive approach to protecting the application.

What Twilio Is Doing to Prevent This from Happening Again

- Restrict direct access to S3 buckets and deliver content
  only over CDNs

- Improve monitoring of S3 bucket policy changes
  to detect changes that could leave their systems
  vulnerable

Restricting direct access to S3 buckets and only delivering content via the CDN can provide a variety of benefits. Aside from protecting from future injection attacks, CDNs can reduce the latency to the customer and reduce the costs associated with cloud computing by limiting the data being transferred out of the S3 bucket.

Twilio did not provide information on how they would be monitoring S3 bucket policies, but one resource that can be used to provide both proactive and reactive measures of protection is AWS Config. Config is used to obtain a detailed view of configuration updates of AWS resources in an AWS account. This review shows how resources are related and configured in the past and how they have changed over time. Config is compatible with several different AWS services including S3 storage service. Config can be used to evaluate the configuration settings of AWS resources and detect if a resource violates the conditions in the rules. Config can send a notification based on the status of the rules.

AWS Config rules are checked and will produce one of the four different results:

1. **COMPLIANT**: The rule passes the condition of the compliance check.

2. **NON_COMPLIANT**: The rule fails the conditions of the compliance check.

3. **ERROR**: One of the parameters is not valid.

4. **NOT_APPLICABLE**: Filtered out resources that a rule cannot be applied to.

If a NON_COMPLIANT result is produced, AWS will flag the resource and rule as noncompliant, and a notification is sent via Amazon Simple Notification Service (SNS).[9]

Look Internally

Security groups, access control lists, and AWS Shield are examples of protection from external threats, but, according to Verizon, 82% of data breaches were from internal threats. These internal threats could be from human errors and innocent mistakes to disgruntled current or former employees whose access is not monitored or revoked. The "human factor" has long been one of the biggest vulnerabilities in technology due to a lack of training, distraction, or malice toward an organization.

---

[9] https://docs.aws.amazon.com/config/latest/developerguide/WhatIsConfig.html

THINK ABOUT IT

Tom was recently caught violating company policy and was terminated from his role at ABC Company. Tom was a senior administrator and early in his career at ABC Company created another user to provide himself an alternative way of accessing an account if his primary credentials were compromised. He never had to use it, and after a particularly bad day of job hunting, he wondered if the secondary user credentials he created were still active. To his surprise, they were and he still had the same level of access as a senior administrator. He changed the settings of the user to not throw any obvious red flags in the audit logs and is now contemplating what he should do next with this access.

What could ABC Company have done to prevent Tom from gaining access? This can be an all-too-common scenario where an authorized person creates an alternative access (a backdoor) with the initial intent of a preventive measure but can be forgotten and remain inconspicuous and active when this person leaves. Some actions that could have been taken are listed as follows:

- Perform regular audits on all user accounts, roles, and groups

- Limit access based on IP addresses

- Use intelligent monitoring to identify any anomalies

Some of the most common types of internal threats do not discriminate between cloud and traditional computing models. These types of threats are[10]

- **Unintentional threats**: These are threats that are due to poor training, negligence, distraction, ignorance of security policies, misplacing a device, or falling victim to a social engineering attack such as opening a phishing email or a dropped USB.

---

[10]`www.cimcor.com/blog/8-examples-of-insider-internal-caused-data-breaches`

- **Intentional threats**: These are threats that aim to cause intentional harm. This can be for personal gain or motives such as being terminated, passed over for a promotion, etc.

- **Collusive threats**: These are threats that come when internal employees work with external attackers to attack an organization.

- **Third-party threats**: These are threats that are not from employees but are granted specific access for a temporary period of time to perform work. Examples of third-party threats include contractors and vendors who have been granted access to specific areas physically or over a network to complete their assigned job.

One of the attacks I first bring to the discussion when teaching about security on AWS is the Capital One Data Breach in 2019. Paige Thompson was a former Amazon.com employee who was able to get past security measures and access unencrypted data stored in S3. (By now, you may have noticed that S3 buckets are a popular target by threat actors.)

Snapchat has also been a victim of social engineering cyberattacks. In 2016, a whaling attack sent emails to Snapchat's human resources personnel posing as the CEO of the company. This phishing email was successful in collecting the personal private information of Snap's employees. This is an excellent example of unintentional threats that, all too often, humans are susceptible to – whether it's driven by fear of reprimand if not performed, the promise of promotion or raises if performed well, etc. When I taught in higher ed, it was not uncommon to receive emails seemingly from the president and vice president of the institution. The CIO and IT team were aware of the attacks and worked to prevent them from reaching their intended audience with appropriate firewalls but also supplemented their efforts by informing the college and all who could receive these emails that these emails were attempts of attack and not to open them, click on any links, or perform any actions they were asked to do.

Cash App

The popular mobile payment service Cash App (a subsidiary of Block, Inc.) was victim to an attack from a former disgruntled employee who downloaded data from over eight million customers. According to UpGuard,[11] the personally identifiable information (PII) taken were the full names of the client and their brokerage account number, values, holdings, and stock trading activity (no evidence of PII data such as dates of birth or social security numbers).

Ironically, a Cash App blog[12] titled "App-Layer Encryption in AWS" was published in 2020. In this article, the authors address the importance of data encryption and the use of services like AWS Key Management Service (KMS) to encrypt data safely and easily, on demand, and as close to data creation as possible. It's not evident in the article what type of data was protected using this service and what data was permitted to remain in plaintext. Recall that in the Capital One Data Breach, some data was stored using encryption, and other PII was stored in plaintext.

In a regulatory filing with the US Securities and Exchange Commission (SEC)[13] on April 4, 2022, it is stated that it was discovered in December 2021 that some data collected from US customers was compromised. The filing stated that the employee had regular access to this data during their employment but, for the time in question, accessed the data without permission due to their employment being terminated. Other PII such as social security numbers, date of birth, credit card information, and addresses were not obtained. Account protection data such as security codes, access codes, and passwords used to access Cash App accounts were also not compromised.

---

[11] www.upguard.com/blog/how-did-the-cash-app-data-breach-happen
[12] https://code.cash.app/app-layer-encryption
[13] www.sec.gov/ix?doc=/Archives/edgar/data/0001512673/000119312522095215/d343042d8k.htm

The takeaway I want you to have from the Cash App security breach is that despite using encryption to protect data from unauthorized access using AWS KMS, the breach was caused by a former employee who had regular access to the data. Although the event history between termination and unauthorized access is not apparent at this time, it can be a good time to review some best practices to avoid a similar event from taking place.

1. **Block, monitor, and audit account access** to any employees who no longer require access. This can be due to project completion or termination. Auditing tools such as AWS CloudTrail and CloudTrail Insights can automate the monitoring.

2. **Use a strong MFA** to prevent simpler MFAs such as short, numerical OTP from being compromised.

3. **Monitor your attack surface** by finding and patching vulnerabilities that can impact business assets and operations.

While Snapchat's leak of employee information was a result of poor social engineering training, the Cash App is an excellent example of best practices that are overlooked even in today's age and knowledge of cyber threats. This attack could have been prevented by adopting some best practices for Identity and Access Management provided by the Security Pillar in the Well-Architected Framework. Some basic best practices to protect accounts from internal threats are as follows:[14]

- **Use strong sign-in mechanisms**

  - Use a strong multifactor authentication (MFA) to reduce the risk of unintended or unauthorized access to credentials.

---

[14] https://docs.aws.amazon.com/wellarchitected/latest/security-pillar/identity-and-access-management.html

- **Use a centralized identity provider**

  - Use an identity provider (IdP) to manage workforce identities in a centralized location that can be used to manage access to multiple accounts and services.

- **Audit and rotate credentials regularly**

  - Limit the life of credentials that can be used to access resources and data.

- **Leverage user groups and their attributes**

  - Organize and manage users into groups based on job function and needed access.

  - Control access at a group level and manage individual access by removing a user from the group to disassociate them from a permission set.

- **Define access requirements**

  - Create a clear definition and timeline for access to a resource or service.

  - Establish a secure method of authentication of the user (i.e., MFA).

- **Grant least privilege access**

  - The principle of least privilege (PoLP) is a foundational security best practice to set permissions based on the minimum needed to perform their job.

- **Define permission guardrails**

  - Establish controls that restrict access to all identities.

- **Analyze public and cross-account access**

  - Monitor and audit findings that show public and cross-account access.

  - Reduce access based on PoLP.

- **Share resource security within the organization**

  - Use Service Control Policies (SCPs).

  - Monitor and audit the use of shared resources continuously.

  - Use automatic notifications when there are unexpected access or configuration changes.

Identify and Implement Change Management/Monitoring Services into the Architecture

- **CloudWatch**: Monitors AWS resources and applications in real time. This is an example of Software as a Service and is automatically enabled for free for one-minute interval checks (Standard resolution). CloudWatch can also be applied at one-second granularity (high resolution). Alarms can be created based on the metrics and send notifications or automatically make changes to resources when a threshold is breached.

  - Monitoring CloudWatch is an example of a proactive measure of identifying anomalies (i.e., DDoS attacks).

- **CloudTrail**:[15] Provides audits of account access and
  API calls in an account. Records actions taken by a
  user, role, or AWS service. Like CloudWatch, it is an
  example of a Software as a Service solution. CloudTrail
  is enabled by default. CloudTrail Insights is an optional
  service that can be used to identify any abnormal
  activity.

  - Auditing CloudTrail is an example of a proactive
    measure of identifying suspicious activity in an
    AWS account.

- **Security Hub**:[16] Provides a comprehensive view of AWS
  accounts' security state and checks the architecture
  environment with best practices. Works with AWS
  accounts, services, and select third-party partner
  products to analyze security trends and the highest
  priority security issues.

- **Config**: Evaluates the configuration settings of the AWS
  resources. There are two different types of Config rules:

  - AWS Config Managed Rules are predefined,
    customizable rules that were created by
    AWS Config.

  - AWS Config Custom Rules are rules created from
    scratch.

---

[15] https://docs.aws.amazon.com/awscloudtrail/latest/userguide/
cloudtrail-user-guide.html

[16] https://docs.aws.amazon.com/securityhub/latest/userguide/what-is-
securityhub.html

Identify and Understand the Costs of Failing to Implement Change Management and Notification Services into the Architecture

The factors that can influence change management are people and their habits, culture, processes, time, and money.

The biggest threat to any cybersecurity system is the human factor. Whether it be due to a lack of training or lack of enforcement of policies, people who fail to break bad habits can lead to missed opportunities for personal and organizational improvement and overall security posture. AWS provides monitoring services at no charge to capture user access and anomalies in services, but using these services and establishing a playbook is required for them to be fully effective. These improvements can result from identifying errors and performing a root cause analysis to discover patterns. The Twilio case mentioned earlier in this chapter is a great example of how an organization realizes that an attack has been made on their infrastructure and, after discovering the issue, performs a check on other services that could face similar configuration errors and adopts a change in their practices to prevent similar errors from happening.

Culture can also be a barrier that prevents change management services from being correctly utilized. Organizations that are slow to adopt cloud computing technologies can be unaware of the change management tools that can be used to proactively protect their infrastructure. Leaders in charge of managing a migration need to be aware of not only the technical aspects of migration but the mental shift as well. AWS's Cloud Adoption Framework is built upon six different perspectives with individual capabilities that can help with stakeholder management and address specific concerns. Changes in processes from the legacy model can create resistance to changes. Notification services like SNS require a user to subscribe to the topic to receive notifications based on changes and follow-through to determine a root cause analysis.

Cloud Security Alert Fatigue

A word of caution on ensuring that notifications are appropriately set up. Notifications can be based on thresholds. Machine learning can help identify a normal range of anomalies based on service, time of event, etc. This can help ensure that thresholds are accurately monitored so as not to unnecessarily spend resources researching triggers. It is important that the human factor is included in these automated notifications. Cloud security alert fatigue can lessen the impact and urgency when alerts are triggered due to ineffective thresholds.

When I was in higher ed, my office was located in an older building with very sensitive smoke detectors. If someone left the popcorn in the microwave a little too long, the fire alarms would go off. Everyone had to evacuate the building although most had become so accustomed and annoyed by it that the fear of a fire was the last thing anyone was concerned about. What would have happened if there was an actual fire? Just like the boy who cried wolf, when an alarm is sounded too often we develop alarm fatigue and will be unlikely to react with the appropriate urgency should a real alarm take place.

Just like alarm fatigue can dull our senses and speed to react in an older building, alert fatigue happens when security professionals are exposed to a large number of alerts (alarms) that are meaningless and not prioritized. The Orca Security 2022 Cloud Security Alert Fatigue Report[17] surveyed over 800 IT professionals with some surprising results:

---

[17] https://orca.security/resources/blog/2022-cloud-cyber-security-alert-fatigue-report/#:~:text=What%20is%20Cloud%20Security%20Alert,different%20in%20public%20cloud%20security

- 59% of those polled receive over 500 cloud security alerts per day.

- 55% of those polled miss critical calls regularly.

- 43% of those polled state that over 40% of those alerts are false positives.

Identify What Ethical Hacking Looks like in the Cloud

Cloud computing has helped bring the fourth industrial revolution in full force. This new phase in technology and its use also brought in a new attack surface – the cyber surface can now be added to air, water, and land as areas of attack.

It is important to remember that cloud computing is based on a Shared Responsibility Model for maintaining security of the cloud and in the cloud. Many cloud computing customers struggle to remember that just because cloud computing is not tangible does not mean that the attack plane is not accessible to attackers. The Shared Responsibility Model states that customers are responsible for security in the cloud, and with the growth of cloud computing adoption and cyberattacks comes the need for businesses to develop defenses to attacks and recovery plans.

Ethical hacking requires many of the same skills as malicious attackers, but they must be mindful and follow laws and organization requirements. Ethical hackers scan cloud computing environments looking for vulnerabilities that can be exploited.[18] Ethical hackers use the same

---

[18] www.eccouncil.org/cybersecurity-exchange/ethical-hacking/ethical-hacking-cloud-computing/

techniques as unethical hackers to detect issues within the infrastructure using approved hacking techniques. It is important that the scope of the attack must be within the laws and organization specifications.

Ethical hackers in cloud computing environments can have the following responsibilities:

- Identifying and patching broken cloud authentication services

- Identifying unintentional exposure of data and files

- Providing suggestions against DDoS

- Protecting systems from malware

Use the Security Pillar Design Principles

The Well-Architected Framework is built on six pillars to build a cloud infrastructure based on best practices. In this chapter, you have seen examples of how organizations like Snap, Volkswagen, and Twilio approach the security of their infrastructure. Some are using services that are intended to find vulnerabilities early before they are exploited, and others are due to misconfigurations due to updates.

The Security Pillar[19] provides a set of design principles that customers can use as a framework to build from and strengthen the security of the workload. The design principles for the Security Pillar are as follows:

- Implement a strong identity foundation that enforces the separation of duties based on a user's needs to perform their job.

- Maintain traceability by using and auditing monitoring services like CloudTrail.

---

[19] https://docs.aws.amazon.com/wellarchitected/latest/security-pillar/security.html

116

- Use a defense-in-depth approach at multiple layers.

- Use automation and managed services.

- Protect data in transit and at rest based on data classification.

- Protect data at the source. Use front-facing endpoints to serve as a proxy to the backend.

- Plan for failures or other security events.

Security requires more than a one-and-done approach. Anything that is built to last needs to be built over a period of time with tests performed and lessons learned about the things that bend and break in our systems.

Summary

Security is a moving target, and many security professionals are overwhelmed with keeping their eyes on all the balls in play. Cloud security posture management (CSPM) like AWS Security Hub and other third-party vendors can provide the benefit of maintaining an overall secure application in a single dashboard. Automation can also be added to these CSPM tools to help reduce alert fatigue and allow more focus and attention on mitigating cyber threats. The design principles of the Security Pillar of the Well-Architected Framework provide best practices to build a secure network based on consistent practices and efforts.

CHAPTER 5

Is This the End?

AWS shared findings from CJ Moses' *Security Predictions for 2023 and Beyond*, and it is a mixture of some expectations and surprises. The six predictions listed are as follows:

1. Security will be integral to everything that organizations do.

2. Diversity will help address the continued security talent gap.

3. Automation driven by AI/ML will enable stronger security.

4. People will drive greater data protection investment.

5. More advanced forms of multifactor authentication will become pervasive.

6. Quantum computing will benefit security.

Is this the end? Yes and no. Yes, this is the final chapter, but this is far from the end in understanding and learning about vulnerabilities and being proactive in your education. In my classes, I reinforce the need to be a lifelong learner. There is no compromise on that tenet in the field of technology. AWS provides multiple resources to not only apply in order to build a more secure infrastructure but also materials to learn how to use them effectively.

© Tasha Penwell 2023
T. Penwell, *Beginning AWS Security*, https://doi.org/10.1007/978-1-4842-9681-3_5

To finish this book, I wanted to bring in the *Security Predictions for 2023 and Beyond* from CJ Moses, the Deputy Chief Information Security Officer and VP of Security Engineering for Amazon Web Services (AWS). In this publication from November 2022, he made six predictions on how cybersecurity will change in not only attacks but how security professionals can prevent and combat those attacks.

Prediction 1: Security Will Be Integral to Everything That Organizations Do

"Data is the new gold" – that's one of the tenets I share with my learners when we start learning about AWS security services. AWS says security is job one, but they also make note that security is a shared responsibility, so it's vital that cloud customers are aware of their responsibilities to maintain data security. **Some projections state that by 2025 there will be 463 exabytes of data.** With this expected influx of data from a variety of sources, customers will need a way to secure data from collection to destruction.

In its Shared Responsibility Model, AWS states that they are responsible for the security of the cloud, and it is the customer's responsibility for security in the cloud. For the customers, this includes duties for managing identities and permissions, protecting networks and infrastructures, identifying and responding to threats, data protection, and demonstrating overall compliance with regional and industry-specific laws and regulations.

AWS cloud computing resources can help offset the mundane activities of logging, monitoring, auditing, and patching by integrating specific services such as IAM.

Moses states that in 2020 people created 1.7 MB of data every second. Some predictions say that by 2025 there will be 463 exabytes of data. This influx of data that is being collected thanks to mobile and web applications, IoT devices, and smart everything has created a deluge of data. Organizations are struggling to parse through, analyze, and learn from the data. Datasets are being stored in data lakes until it can be better used and utilized. This influx of data is one of the reasons that the cloud is becoming more widely adopted.

Despite the ability to offset the management of infrastructure to the cloud, the security of the data is still the responsibility of those who own the data. Remember, AWS does not take ownership of the data – it is still your data, it's just stored on their infrastructure. This can be done by managing the groups, roles, and users who have access to data stores and data sources. Maintaining effective security policies includes the following:

- Managing identities and permissions

- Protecting the network and infrastructure (based on your services and cloud model)

- Identifying and responding to threats

- Data protection policies

- Demonstrating compliance with your industry and/or governmental laws

Cloud computing can automate mundane tasks like logging, monitoring, auditing, patching, and integrating with the existing toolset. Despite the mundaneness of it, knowing and identifying any actions taking place in your AWS account is a key factor of security and maintaining operational best practices. The following are services that are natively provided by AWS to help organizations readily secure their applications and identify any anomalies:

- Identity and Access Management (IAM)

  - Free service with AWS

  - Provides you with the resources to manage who can access what resource at a granular level

- Operates on implicit denial unless explicitly allowed

- Can be granted to services, users, groups, and roles

- Supports MFA

- Works with CloudTrail to create logs of who is making requests in the account

- CloudTrail

  - Free service with AWS that is automatically enabled

  - Used for operation and risk auditing

  - Helps support governance and account compliance

  - Actions taken by a user, role, or an AWS service are recorded as events

- Key Management Service (KMS)

  - Managed service that supports you in creating and controlling the keys used to protect your data

  - Integrates with most other services to encrypt your data

- Web Application Firewall (WAF)

  - Supports you in monitoring HTTP(S) requests sent to your web application resources

- GuardDuty

  - Security monitoring service

  - Analyzes and processes data sources from CloudTrail, VPC flow logs, DNS logs, and more

- Uses threat intelligence that includes lists of malicious IP addresses and domains to identify potential attacks

- Uses machine learning to identify potentially malicious activity in the account

- Security Hub

  - Provides an overall view of your account's security posture

  - Checks the environment against security standards and best practices

  - Provides a consolidated view of security findings across accounts and provider products

  - Integrates with EventBridge to automate remediation findings

- Inspector

  - Vulnerability management service

  - Scans workloads in AWS for vulnerabilities in the software

  - Automatically discovers and performs scans on EC2 instances, container images in ECR, and Lambda functions

  - Findings are generated from vulnerabilities discovered during the scans

- Systems Manager

  - Centralizes operational data from multiple AWS services

  - Automates tasks across resources on AWS

  - Provides a central place to view and manage resources on AWS and in a multicloud environment

- EventBridge

  - Serverless service

  - Event-based service that applies rules to a target when triggered

Prediction 2: Diversity Will Help Address the Continued Security Talent Gap

Over the years, there has been an increased focus on developing DEI (diversity, equity, and inclusion) in the workforce. The goal of DEI is to promote fair treatment and full participation of all individuals. While the characteristics that are often used to describe DEI are gender, race, and sexual orientation, the goal is to find talent. Removing barriers to opportunities allows for talent and experience to enter the cybersecurity workforce from diverse socioeconomic backgrounds. This diversity allows for new ideas, new methods, and various experiences to enter the mix.

As cloud adoption increases, so do the vulnerabilities and new techniques in attacks. This has seen a large growth in the need for security professionals from different backgrounds and capabilities. Organizations are taking advantage of the diverse talent set that shows skills and initiative even without the traditional college degree. Taking advantage of populations that are neurodiverse or have different cultures and backgrounds can be beneficial by bringing nontraditional thinking to solve security threats proactively.

Both the *Harvard Business Review*[1] and the *Australian Cyber Security Magazine*[2] have written about the special talents that neurodiverse security specialists have to protect from attacks.

When I'm teaching about AWS, it is a great experience for everyone in the class when you have a diverse group of learners with varying backgrounds. All can contribute to the conversation and learning experience by bringing their own questions, experience, and unique perspectives. Half of the battle in technology is having the right mindset when it comes to change and failures, so it is imperative that cloud security specialists (and anyone else in tech) have the right attitude for success. When I've worked with recruiters and inquired about what skills they needed the most from the learners I was teaching; they said they are willing to hire entry-level roles without all the skills as long as they are willing to learn and have the right attitude. The only constant with technology is that it is ever changing. The attitude and aptitude to grow and pivot with those changes can be instrumental in a career.

Prediction 3: Automation Driven by AI/ML Will Enable Stronger Security

Before we dive into what artificial intelligence and machine learning can do for cybersecurity, let's spend some time learning what these technologies are. The terms are often used interchangeably because they work in tandem, but they do have some distinctive qualities.

---

[1] https://hbr.org/2017/05/neurodiversity-as-a-competitive-advantage
[2] https://australiancybersecuritymagazine.com.au/where-autism-offers-a-competitive-advantage/

Artificial intelligence is the ability of a computing device to imitate human intelligence. Remember, computers are innately dumb and will only perform the tasks you tell them. They do not have the reason or logic to make decisions on how to carry out instructions. With AI, that is changing. Machines are able to make logical decisions that imitate human behavior. Computing devices are capable of doing things like problem-solving, learning, and adjusting as needed based on events. This is made capable by a set of technologies that are implemented in it.

Machine learning is a subset of AI. It enables a machine or a system to learn and improve from experience. Machine learning relies less on manual programming efforts and more on algorithms used to analyze large datasets and learn from the information derived from the data to make informed decisions.

To sum it up, AI is the broad usage of using machines and systems to develop artificial senses, reasoning, and adapt as a human would. Machine learning is a narrower focus of using AI. It helps machines gain knowledge from data and learn about it with little to no human interaction.

According to BitLyft,[3] cyberattackers are exploiting vulnerabilities that are being created through unsecured practices in remote work, cloud deployment gaps, and digital transformations that are leaving security gaps.

The unfortunate truth is that IaaS, PaaS, and SaaS are not the only types of _aaS that cloud specialists need to be familiar with. Ransomware as a Service is a big threat that uses AI technologies to gain access to networks and attacks. Cybersecurity professionals must fight fire with fire by using their own tools that utilize AI and ML to improve their overall security posture.

---

[3] https://www.bitlyft.com/resources/ai-and-machine-learning-harnessing-the-power-of-automation

Data provided from Meticulous Research[4] shares the following:

- Cybersecurity-as-a-Service Market will be worth $46.6 billion by 2030.

- Automotive Cybersecurity Market will be worth $13.9 billion by 2030.

- Cybersecurity Services Market will be worth $158.4 billion by 2030.

- Industrial Cybersecurity Market will be worth $49.53 billion by 2030.

- Healthcare Cybersecurity Market will be worth $26.1 billion by 2027.

- Cybersecurity Market is bolstering its growth to exceed $300 billion by 2027.

- Rising adoption IoT and Cyberattacks fuels growth of AI in the security.

Meticulous Research[5] reported that the rising adoption of IoT and cyberattacks has spawned the growth of using AI in cybersecurity. AI and ML can be used to develop preventative and reactive measures against attacks by performing the following:

- Threat and attack detection

- Reduction of alert fatigue

- Identification of zero-day exploits

- Attack and alert response

- Elimination of manual tasks

---

[4] www.meticulousresearch.com/pressrelease-store
[5] www.meticulousresearch.com/pressrelease/159/artificial-intelligence-in-security-market

IBM's data breach action guide[6] report reinforces the need to learn from data breaches. It is important to develop protocols for threat detection. AWS's Well-Architected Framework has an entire pillar devoted to developing best habits and following protocols to prevent attacks and respond to a threat.

Incorporating machine learning and artificial intelligence, organizations can improve their defense-in-depth approach by adding another layer that can be used to protect the infrastructure and allow developers to focus on their application. In a short interview with Robert Zou from Snap, Robert states that using machine learning–enabled tools such as Amazon GuardDuty allows them to focus on their application and less time focusing on security.

In addition to GuardDuty, AWS also provides the following machine learning–enabled services:

- Amazon Detective[7]

    - Helps you perform a root cause analysis on any security concerns

    - Uses machine learning and log data to allow you to perform quick analysis

- Amazon CodeGuru Security

    - Creates security policies based on best practices from Amazon.com and AWS

    - Proactively scans and detects security violations and vulnerabilities and suggests improvements

---

[6] www.ibm.com/reports/data-breach-action-guide
[7] https://docs.aws.amazon.com/detective/latest/adminguide/what-is-detective.html

- Macie

  - Data security service that uses machine learning to identify patterns

  - Helps provide visibility of data risks and automates protections against those risks

One of the largest vulnerabilities that organizations face is the people. Intentional or unintentional, failure to maintain a policy of the principle of least privilege or monitor logs can not only create a security threat but also create unnecessary costs related to unmanaged access to create resources that do not follow an organization's security policy. AWS services like Audit Manager and IAM Access Analyzer can help you continuously audit your AWS usage to simplify how you assess risk and compliance with regulations and industry standards. Audit Manager can be used to ensure that policies and procedures are being correctly followed. IAM Access Analyzer helps identify access to resources shared with an external entity is meeting least privilege guidelines.

Prediction 4: People Will Drive Greater Data Protection Investment

Laws, regulations, or bad press are oftentimes what causes a change in data protection. Data protection can be difficult throughout all the stages of the data lifecycle – from acquisition to destruction/archival. Many times, if the data collection is known, data classifications can help automate the processes.

As data is becoming more of a primary concern for all countries, states, counties, and cities, so do more laws go into effect. Gartner published a report that identified the Top Five Trends in Privacy Through 2024.[8]

According to Nader Henein, VP Analyst at Gartner, it is predicted that more than 75% of the world's population will have its personal data covered under modern privacy regulations. This wave will be the driving force for organizations that do not currently have a dedicated policy to practice privacy; the responsibility of maintaining privacy is passed to the technology that is used (such as the cloud).

The five privacy trends that support the best practices to support data privacy and make this an attainable goal are the following:

1. Data Localization

2. Privacy-Enhancing Computation Techniques

3. AI Governance

4. Centralized Privacy UX

5. Remote Becomes "Hybrid Everything"

Data Localization

Data localization focuses on the residency of data. This includes both the storage and processing of data and the laws that govern both the geographical areas and industry.

Privacy-Enhancing Computation Techniques

Privacy-enhancing computation techniques are technologies that work together to ensure high security of data.

---

[8] www.gartner.com/en/newsroom/press-releases/2022-05-31-gartner-identifies-top-five-trends-in-privacy-through-2024

AI Governance

Artificial intelligence governance helps ensure that research and growing use cases of AI and ML are for the benefit of society. I think most people would agree the *Terminator* movie is not something we would want to see come to life.

Centralized Privacy UX

Most Internet users understand that privacy can be potentially compromised by simply accessing the Web. It is becoming more of a contention and consumers are expecting more efforts to protect their data privacy.

Remote Becomes "Hybrid Everything"

When Covid-19 required everything to go remote in a hurry, it created many last-minute decisions as businesses and schools worked to support remote everything. As months and years have gone by, many organizations have adjusted to seeing value in both on-site and off-site environments. Different organizations must adhere to the requirements on how to provide secure access between resources needed on- and off-site.

With this greater demand and expectation for privacy protection will come increased laws and regulations. Organizations that are proactively taking advantage of resources to secure the network must ensure that a budget is set to support protection and threat detection. This is an ongoing assessment of what organizations are responsible for doing. Tools like IAM, CloudTrail, and Macie can be used to determine any potential issues of data security or who has access to it.

Prediction 5: More Advanced Forms of MFA Will Become Pervasive

MFA is becoming not only a best practice but a requirement – and with good reason. As organizations are expected to shoulder the responsibility of compromised data in the cloud, there needs to be an enforced due diligence on the part of users. Passwords are a burden that most of us hate, and if you don't hate them, it may be because they are not as secure as they should be. Passwords are inconvenient to put it mildly. The best practice of not reusing passwords for different platforms when you take into account the number of platforms we use on a daily basis is laughable. These reasons and many more are why passwordless is coming in exchange for a passkey.

Passkeys replace the need for something you attempt to remember in exchange for something that is harder to replicate or steal because it is based on a possession you have or a biometric characteristic that is unique to you. While the attempt to walk away from passwords to passkeys has been long in wanting, the transition took much longer in large part due to the legacy applications and frameworks that were not equipped to handle this change. As more organizations are adopting cloud computing to their infrastructure, it allows these organizations to build an application and infrastructure that will support enforcing millions of users taking actions to protect their own data.

Prediction 6: Quantum Computing Will Benefit Security

Quantum computing, in simple terms, is the process where computers rely on qubits to solve very advanced and complex algorithms. A qubit is a basic unit of information similar to the bit in more commonly used computing. A qubit stores information, but because it is used for quantum computing, it behaves differently.

Access to quantum computing today is not as readily available as the computing devices we use today. While different factors play into it, access to quantum computing today is similar to access to home computers in the 1950s. According to the Quantum Insider, a quantum computer in 2023 could run you $15 million.

While quantum computing is not readily accessible yet, that does not mean it is not being used – thanks to cloud services that are available. Remember – infrastructures are available for use with the cloud with no commitment to buy.

Knowing the speed at which quantum computing can work, security standards will need to change. Remember that security is about staying in front of the ball – not watching it go past you – so while quantum computing may not be breaking encryption keys yet, we need to predict where they will be when they do.

This type of power is not meant to be used to collect data that is perishable and easily changed. Instead, the focus is on the vulnerability of data that needs to be protected from inception to destruction – if it is ever destroyed.

CJ Moses' prediction that security will be integrated into everything an organization does is not earth-shattering. Large organizations to individuals understand that security is an important part of our daily lives.

I remember when I was trying to add my stepson to my health insurance plan and needed his social security number. He knew not to send it to me via text or messenger. The world provides us with news stories of why security is paramount at every level, and every person has a responsibility to maintain it.

Cryptograph Standards

As technologies change and expectations rise, the cryptography standards used will need to also evolve. Quantum computing is a great example of how changing computing power and resources requires more effort and forethought on how to secure networks and applications.

The National Institute of Standards and Technology (NIST)[9] is currently working on Post-Quantum Cryptography (PQC). The NIST is working with cryptographers and accepting proposals for quantum-resistant cryptography. As the NIST describes it, this is a preemptive measure if large-scale quantum computers are ever built and can break today's cryptographic systems. The goal of PQC is to develop cryptographic systems that can withstand attacks from quantum-powered computers while using current protocols and networks.

In true AWS fashion, they are not left behind on this mission for PQC. The research team is focusing on improving security options for both managed and unmanaged services for the customers.[10] Security is job one at AWS, and the future of technology is not going to change that.

In fact, AWS Key Management Service (KMS) and AWS Certificate Manager (ACM) support the latest hybrid post-quantum Transport Layer Security (TLS) ciphers. This TLS configuration uses a key encapsulation mechanism created from NIST's PQC Round 3 selection process.[11]

---

[9] https://csrc.nist.gov/projects/post-quantum-cryptography
[10] https://aws.amazon.com/security/post-quantum-cryptography/
[11] https://aws.amazon.com/about-aws/whats-new/2022/03/aws-kms-acm-support-latest-hybrid-post-quantum-tls-ciphers/

In May 2022, the White House launched the National Security Memorandum on Promoting United States Leadership in Quantum Computing While Mitigating Risks to Vulnerable Cryptographic Systems.[12] In this memorandum, it states that with the benefits that can be derived from quantum computing, there are also pitfalls due to its increased speed and size it could break the public-key cryptography.

To answer the question at the beginning, this is not the end. In fact, the more you learn about the vulnerabilities and advancements in technologies, you may see things as I do – that more knowledge on vulnerabilities means more tools and techniques to learn. The security predictions we visited throughout this chapter we have already seen coming true. Some are for the good, such as increased focus on security and realizing the abilities and skills of the neurodiverse can be a strength. Some are, admittedly, a little terrifying.

Before we finish this book out, I would like to reinforce two things:

1. Shared Responsibility Model

2. Well-Architected Framework

These two resources with AWS provide you foundational knowledge on how to maintain a highly secure environment.

The Shared Responsibility Model provides a definition of who is responsible for security based on "security of the cloud" vs. "security in the cloud."

---

[12] www.whitehouse.gov/briefing-room/statements-releases/2022/05/04/
national-security-memorandum-on-promoting-united-states-leadership-
in-quantum-computing-while-mitigating-risks-to-vulnerable-
cryptographic-systems/

The Well-Architected Framework is used to build on the six foundational pillars. These pillars provide guidance to build an environment using best practices to maintain performance, reliability, operation, costs, security, and sustainability. The Security Pillar focuses on seven areas:

1. Security foundations

2. Identity and access management

3. Detection

4. Infrastructure protection

5. Data protection

6. Incident response

7. Application security

Summary

Lifelong learning is a lifelong adventure. When asking about my teaching philosophy, my answer is simple – learning should be fun. Learning is a skill that requires patience, practice, and resources. Security is a fascinating and challenging topic to continue to grow your knowledge and skills. Resources that you can take advantage of at no charge are listed as follows:

- AWS Educate: `https://aws.amazon.com/education/awseducate/`

- AWS Skill Builder: `https://explore.skillbuilder.aws/`

- AWS Ramp-Up Guides: `https://d1.awsstatic.com/training-and-certification/ramp-up_guides/Ramp-Up_Guide_Security.pdf`

The end of this chapter and this book is not the end of your learning. Continue to grow your skills in an ever-changing, ever-growing industry.

Index

A

Accenture, 5, 20, 21, 23, 69, 72
Access control list (ACL), 25
Access management, 55, 109
Amazon Cognito, 68–69, 72, 84
Amazon Config, 80, 83, 85
Amazon Detective, 65, 70,
          83, 86, 128
Amazon Inspector, 30, 67, 70, 80,
          82, 83, 85
Amazon Macie, 30, 31, 68, 71, 81, 89
Amazon Web Services (AWS), 120
App-Layer Encryption in AWS
          (Cash App blog), 108
Application security, 77, 78, 83
Artificial intelligence, 27,
          125–128, 131
Asset
     automation, 98
     location, 97
     unmonitored and
          unprotected, 97
Attacker, 4, 42, 87–90, 102, 115
Automate security, 12, 54, 88
AWS
     customers, 7, 72
     data centers, 2

protection, 14
resources, 79
responsibility, 15
security, 1, 2
security pillar's design
          principles, 88–90
security resources, 69
security resources and
          pricing, 8, 9
security services and
          pricing, 8, 9
services, 16, 17, 63, 70–72
vulnerabilities, 32
well-architected framework
     cloud architecture, 11
     pillars, 10, 11
     security, 12
     Security Pillar, 11
     trade-offs, 10, 11
AWS Cloud Security
          documentation, 38
AWS Config, 23, 24, 30, 31, 68, 71,
          86, 104, 105
AWS Config Managed
          Rules, 25, 112
AWS's Cloud Adoption
          Framework, 73, 113

© Tasha Penwell 2023
T. Penwell, *Beginning AWS Security*, https://doi.org/10.1007/978-1-4842-9681-3